Hush Hush
and Other Veneers

Hush Hush and Other Veneers: a memoir

Copyright ©2013 Alexandra Dell'Amore

ISBN: 978-0-9892882-8-6

Publisher: Mercury HeartLink

Albuquerque, New Mexico

Printed in the United States of America

Cover Painting "Ann Street, N.Y.C."
by Alexandra Dell'Amore

Portrait Photography by Tony Louderbough
www.tonylouderbough.com

Contact the author at *taosalex@swcp.com*

Mercury HeartLink
www.heartlink.com

Hush Hush

and Other Veneers

a memoir

Alexandra Dell'Amore

Contents

ACKNOWLEDGEMENTS

My Editors: David L. Brown and Bob Gassaway

Consultant, Linda Sperling

Those who encouraged and helped me:

Joanne Bodin

Mary Dilberger

Jean Green

Pat Heller

Mary Ann Holton

Karin Fredrickson

Anthony Louderbough

Jean Morsch

Ming Moy

Maggi Petton

Rhoda Schlamm

Stewart S. Warren

Adrienne Wing

To my brother, Robert B. Hauck

PREFACE

I wrote my story so readers might understand the diabolical evil I experienced as a child and how I coped with those terrible experiences. In the end, I survived and in a way thrived. I am not unique. It is my hope that adults listen seriously to children and investigate their tales to find out if they are true.

I was born in 1941 Sandra Elliott Hauck to Virginia and Anthony M. Hauck Jr. My father had been the county prosecutor for the famous Lindbergh-Hauptmann trial. Before her marriage my mother worked as an efficiency expert. After her marriage she gave up her career to become a wife and a mother. I was the last child, and the only girl, with three brothers. When I was born, our family lived in a modest house in Hampton, New Jersey. I hope my book will be an interesting journey.

Chapter One

THE BEGINNING

I remember very clearly when, at the age of eight, I was infected with a venereal disease by a man my parents called "doctor." My brothers were away at school when I first met him and his wife. It was in the fall of 1949. I had been in the living room playing checkers on the cobbler's bench with Lulu, our house-keeper. The cold wind howled outside, sending gusts down the chimney, pushing sparks and ashes out of the hearth. The moist cold brushed my cheeks. Doors rattled; the organdy curtains shifted. Lulu said, "Something strange is in the air. Can you smell it?"

"No," I said, as I jumped my checker to make a king.

After dinner that night, my parents drove to town to have a "drink" celebrating a court case my father had won. We heard a car.

"I bet they're back." Lulu rose to see, as the door bashed open with a bang. Icy wind invaded the room. I rushed to greet my parents, but others stood there instead. A short blue-eyed man entered carrying a leather bag. Thick, nearsighted glasses shielded icy eyes. A waxed mustache with horns crossed his upper lip. He greeted me with a peculiar accent, "Hello girlie." Squeezing in beside him was a large woman bundled in brown.

My mother ecstatically introduced the newcomers. The Stoeltings were staying at the Clinton House because their car had broken down. My parents invited them to stay until it was repaired. Dr. Thomas Stoelting, and his wife, Georgie, eagerly accepted. The doctor was a mining engineer searching for investors. He claimed he was German and had graduated from Heidelberg University. Georgie was from California. The couple lived in Boulder Creek, California.

My mother's nod cued me. I introduced myself, "I'm Sandy, and this is Lulu." The doctor held out his hand, "Hello, little girlie." He squinted through his round gold-wire-rimmed glasses. As I shook his hand, I felt an odd tingle from my hand to my throat. I should have paid attention to this. His wife shook my hand, too. Her "Hi" sounded pleasant.

Lulu advanced, taking coats and luggage, then rushed upstairs to make a bedroom ready.

After touring the house, the doctor sat opposite, staring at me. His wife sat next to me, near the fire, smoking a cigarette. My mother called me to bed. "Nice to meet you," I blurted, as I bounded up the stairs.

The next morning, I awoke to voices in the dining room. I jumped up to dress for breakfast. The wide pine boards were frigid to my bare feet as I raced to the bathroom. Snow whirled against the window panes and over the yard. I pulled on my slipper socks, hopped into a skirt and fought into a sweater. My mother came up the stairs as I started down.

"Wait a minute young lady. You can't go down stairs without your hair braided." There was no argument. My hair was braided and tied with bows.

Lulu was busy frying bacon and eggs. A pile of toast sat in the middle of the long dining table. I sat facing the Stoeltings. I was now studying the doctor as he spoke about money and mining claims. "The Great Northern mercury mine will make thousands for investors," he told my father. "Hundreds returned on the dollar. I can sell you stock, if you want to invest."

I understood my father was interested by the way he listened and smiled.

The doctor cut his bacon with a small yellow-handled

pocket knife that squeaked its way across his plate. He grasped the fork upside down before securing the bacon with a stab. My parents didn't notice. I would never be allowed to eat like that.

Georgie wore a fossil agate necklace and ring. This seemed exotic compared to my mother's diamonds and aquamarines. Her long fingers with tapered red nails moved like spider legs as she lighted a cigarette. I fled to the kitchen to find out what Lulu thought. "Don't ask me," she said. I took this to mean she hadn't yet made up her mind.

Later, Georgie told me about California. There, redwood trees were so wide people could drive or walk through tunnels cut through them. She offered to send me some seeds. I liked these people.

Soon, friends were invited to meet the fascinating couple. Medical doctors, members of the bridge club, the gun club and church members came. The "doctor" shot pictures of them with a 3-D Stereo-Realist camera. He and his wife were unusual to our small town culture.

Lulu and my mother were busy cleaning. My mother hired a "girl" from the local reformatory for three dollars a day. The three scrubbed, waxed and ironed. They dug out corner dirt with discarded toothbrushes. They polished the silver with pink paste. The house was clean at all times for possible guests.

The Stoeltings stayed for several months, even after their car was fixed. They slept in my brother's room because he was at college.

About a month after they arrived, I raced up the winding back stairs to visit. Georgie was large and buxom. She lay shoeless on the bed. I stood by the doctor as he sat at the desk in uniform-like khakis. Papers and a map covered the desk top. He had been smoking a pipe. "You know I'm a doctor."

"Yes," I said. "I know."

"I have a special secret to show you," he said in an accented whisper. As he turned, he narrowed his eyes to knife-like slits. Like magic, his upper black lashes formed his blue eyes into black onyx circles.

His chair scraped back noisily as he got up to shut the bedroom door. He nodded knowingly toward Georgie. A sneer spread under his waxed mustache that curved up into horns on each side. He reeked of 4711 cologne.

"Come up here." Georgie whispered in her deep, raspy, cigarette voice. I scrambled up onto the high bed.

The doctor said, "I have a turtle that wants to see your girlie parts." He opened his pants and showed me his penis.

"That's not a turtle, that's a penis," I said. "Where is the turtle?"

Georgie laughed and repeated my question. "Take off your panties so you can see the turtle." She helped me. I was curious to see where the turtle might be.

She held my legs apart while the doctor inserted himself inside me.

"Ouch, that hurts! Don't do that!" I cried but he continued, then withdrew.

"Shush!" Georgie said. I grabbed my pants and pulled them up. I jumped down, running to the door, but the doctor grabbed me about my waist.

"There's no turtle. It's a penis," I blurted. My chapped cheeks burned as I wiped my tears with my sleeves and hands." It's a penis."

Georgie spoke softly. "It really was as turtle, you just didn't see it."

"Then where is it?"

"It went to sleep, and can't come out," the doctor said.

"It's a secret," said Georgie. "Remember it's a secret."

They coaxed me to stay in the room, where they talked to me, and I looked at magazines, before it was "Okay" for me to leave. "Remember, it's a secret." Georgie said one more time.

"I remember, it's a secret."

Of course I told, but not to my mother's liking. We were in the bathroom. I told her the couple had tried to fool me with the turtle story. She looked sad for a moment before announcing, "That's a lie. That couldn't be." I was shocked and confused at her response.

"It was a lie," I agreed. I had upset her. I stood silent for a few moments. Then retracted my statement.

"I told you the truth the first time. He really did put his penis inside me." I pointed to my crotch. She perched her thin body on the side of the tub. She attempted to get up, then shook my shoulders, saying, "You're driving me crazy." She looked at me balefully, pursed her lips and walked out.

Left alone, I stared at a large baby oil bottle standing on the porcelain toilet cover. It was greasy with a pink plastic top. I tried to spell oil, so I could remember. Was it O-I-L, or I-O-L? I was dazed. She did not believe me. I thought I had to do something so she wouldn't be upset, but I was at a loss. I wanted a hug. My mother didn't understand me. It really happened. There was something about a lie and the truth I didn't know. Confusion filled me. I thought I might have spoken wrongly. Otherwise, my mother would know I was truthful. I was missing something.

Days later, my mother stood at her dresser, placing tortoise shell combs in her hair and dabbing on perfume. I stood watching. "What's wrong? she asked. I grasped her hand and led her into the bathroom. "Look," I showed her my yellowish, pink discharge on my underpants.

She said nothing, then rushed downstairs to phone someone.

The next day she nervously drove me to Dr. Hance's office in Easton, Pennsylvania. He was a tall and gruff gynecologist. A brown tweed suit hid under his long white jacket. He glanced at me once after having a "look" then took a sample from my private parts. I waited in the dreary, cold outer room with its dark floors and musty drapes. My mother emerged with a box of special droppers and medicine to instill inside me twice a day. I had gonorrhea.

"Preposterous! I will not be tested for V.D., nor will my wife. You have women come from the reformatory to clean. She could have gotten that from a toilet seat," Stoelting growled, clenching his teeth on his pipe. Then in a soft voice with an edge like a razor, he said, "Little girls tell lies."

"Well, Dr. Hance suggested everyone get tested," my mother returned.

Our family, including my three brothers who were home on vacation, and our housekeeper, Lulu were tested and found negative for disease. The Stoeltings were not tested for disease. It was decreed that I got gonorrhea from a toilet seat. I was treated with an iodine solution for several weeks and cured. For me the incident, although not discussed, was not forgotten. Stoelting was reassured of his power to influence our family.

Christmas came while the Stoeltings visited. I got a doll dressed in pink and a game of Pegity. Our family was happy. My older brother, Tony, home on vacation was intrigued by the doctor. He became interested in mining and geology.

Thomas Stoelting showed me how to curtsy. He signaled when I should perform. Guests thought this was cute. My mother embraced it as good manners. I dreaded to do what he asked me to do. I was frequently fetching something for him from my brother's room, such as his pipe or tobacco. Worse, was when I was made to sit next to him and listen to him talk about mining to the "grown-ups." I was supposed to learn something about mining from him. My parents allowed his control and thought it was good for me. He was a doctor and they believed he was right.

My parents' close friends visited often to meet with Stoelting and his wife. They included doctors: Boyer, Coleman, (both medical doctors) and Hance, the gynecologist and surgeon who treated my gonorrhea, and who would treat me again in the future. The couples had played bridge, gone on trips with my parents, or had treated the family's medical ailments. The men had hunted with my father. The Stoeltings told wonderful stories about mines and easy money. The doctor claimed to be an expert mining engineer. My parents invested in his ventures and supported his mother-in-law and children left in Boulder Creek. They continued supporting the Stoelting family for many years to come.

Stock investments in the Great Northern Mine, a mercury mine, were bought by friends. It was an elite proposition. My father, because he was a lawyer, handled the legal details of incorporating a new company for Stoelting. The couple returned to California after several months. My father sent money; my mother, Virginia, knitted articles and put grocery money aside for them.

When Dr. Stoelting and his wife Georgie raped me in my brother's bedroom, it was the first time I had been tricked. Although I was eight years old, I learned that a lie is a trick. The feeling of being tricked was reinforced by my mother's response to me when she told me, "That's a lie."

This confused me.

Chapter Two

EARLY LIFE

I had a wonderful life on our farm before Dr. Stoelting and his wife came into my life. I was four years old in 1946 when we moved to the farm. It was almost dark as we sped along the dirt road to a steep hilltop. I stood up in the back of our old Ford car and pressed my chin against the scratchy back of the front seat. I wanted to see our new home. My father had bought a large farm near the town of Clinton, New Jersey. Because it was on a hill, we named it Gay Hill Farm. It was the largest house I had ever seen. I ran from room to room exploring all eighteen. There were two living rooms with fireplaces, five bedrooms, an attic the length of the house, and basement servant quarters whose high windows overlooked the front lawn.

A soapstone sink and a Bendix washing machine were on one side of the basement. Two bins of coal and an expansive furnace heated radiators, which made booming sounds in the pipes as they warmed. The smells of soap and coal dust spoke adventure.

The openings to the bins were boarded from the floor up by wooden slats to keep the coal from spilling out. The coal was shiny and inviting. I quickly stepped over the wood to find myself sinking up to my knees. After scrambling out, I was covered with black dust. My mother was furious and made me promise I would never do that again.

The basement hall ended at a thickset door to the outside. Two cozy bedrooms for servants and a shower bath near the furnace remained warm in winter.

The bathroom's wooden door latched with a dark brown

glass handle. A lone, dusty light bulb hung above a small triangular sink. A pull chain and small porcelain fob dangled before a cheap mirror. The gray dingy Masonite walls and damp shower always smelled like wet mud.

Cabinets lined the walls under the stairs awaiting mason jars of garden vegetables. One summer, my mother filled them with a thousand jars of canned vegetables from our garden.

Lulu Taylor, our housekeeper, and Walter Haines, the "outside man," lived in the cellar quarters. A Dutch oven with an iron door was in the wall in Lulu's room. Her room was most likely used as a kitchen in the 1850s when the house was built. We never used the oven for cooking, but it seemed like a wonderful place to hide things. A small window with starched, white cotton curtains opened at eye level. A bright orange-and-brown blanket and several pillows covered Lulu's simple iron bed. The smell of Chesterfield cigarettes and pomade pervaded the air.

Mornings, she slathered baby oil on her silky brown skin and greased her hair before cloaking it in a knotted stocking cap. This she wore until dinner time, when she popped it off into a pocket, exposing her short glistening black hair.

When Lulu was shelling peas or peeling vegetables, I would often run at her to bury my head in her soft abdomen. I learned at an early age that my mother was too busy for such nonsense.

Walter, a tall, quiet man, was part Mohawk. He farmed, cut grass and collected various woods for smoking our hams. After dinner, which he ate in the kitchen, he retired to his room. There he listened to the radio, read or played cards with my brother Bob.

My father, Anthony Hauck Jr., a lawyer, liked farming. He and my three older brothers got busy getting the farm in working order, while my mother planted a garden.

Soon, the chicken coop filled with Leghorns, three pigs ran

muddy in a sty and three sheep lazed in the back corral under an apple tree. Every few days the pigs managed to gleefully rut out to scurry about the fields. My father wanted the pigs to have nose rings to prevent them from escaping. I watched as my three brothers caught the smelly porkers and put rings in their noses. After catching a pig, one brother straddled it while another pressed the ring pliers into the pig's nose and squeezed. Pigs and boys slipped and slid in the muddy, shit-ridden pen. After what to me seemed like hours, our three pigs were sporting new copper rings in their noses. My brothers were covered with mud, pig manure and scratches. The pigs had their revenge. Although they continued to rut in the dirt and against the fence, they didn't rut out as they once had done.

When we first arrived at the farm, draft horses filled the pastures. They weren't ours, but that didn't stop me from embracing them. They were gentle creatures. I'd run out to the field to the nearest one and stand under its furry chest. I'd plant my feet on top of the front hooves, wrap my arms around its sturdy legs and rub the back of my head against its chest. They'd put up with my behavior and didn't walk off. This was a favorite pass time.

"Jean, she's going to get killed," my father shouted at my mother. "She's out here under a horse."

"Well, what do you want me to do?" she retorted. "You're the one who's there."

My father would then admonish me for this behavior. I loved these horses and it was too much fun not to do it again. My mother was often too busy to keep track of me.

We bought the farm from Lloyd Wescott with the agreement that he could keep his horses at our farm for a year. He had horses so he could collect their urine when they were pregnant. The urine was used to make Premarin (PREgnant MARes urINe). Premarin is a hormone manufactured as a replacement for the female hormone, estrogen.

The mares were trained to urinate when led into a box stall filled knee deep in fresh straw. A horse person knows if you take a horse into a stall with fresh straw, it will pee.

After being bred, the mares were tested for pregnancy. The newly pregnant ones were placed at one end of the barn in a large box stall. Bill Miller and Bert Coon or other workers trained them for collection. When one of them was about to pee, a man yelled, "HAAH" and waved a broom at her to make her stop.

The mare was then quickly led to the large collecting stall bedded with fresh straw. The worker whistled while she was led in circles. When the horse urinated, the urine was collected in a pail and then transferred into a large wooden barrel at the side. Filled barrels were trucked to Baker Chemical in Pennsylvania for hormonal processing.

After the collection, the man took her to the entrance of the barn where she drank water from a bath tub trough and was given a hand full of horse feed or bran as a treat.

She was praised, "Good girl, good girl," then led back to her stall.

The training period took about two weeks. The mares soon realized their urine was going to be collected regularly every six hours with a reward.

Next the mares were stabled in standing stalls near the collection area. As a horse became adapted to the routine, she gained more freedom. Eventually these gals were put out to pasture; they would line up at the barn door about every five or six hours for urine collection and a treat.

To a kid, the barn smells of horses, feed and hay were wonderful.

People visited to see the horses and learn how the business was managed. I would dash ahead to show them the huge horses and tell the people the horses' names.

After Wescott took back his horses, we bought our own. Urine was sold for a dollar a gallon. Men worked in shifts around the clock, so the horses didn't have to wait too long to urinate. A small office at the side of the barn's loft stairs held breeding records and a springy, brown bed with a scratchy cover. The night workers used this for napping.

We built a stallion barn for two or three stallions to keep the mares in foal. One was an army remount stallion, King Sandan, who was lent to us from the government. The government wanted to improve the quality of horses in the U.S. During WWII. The Americans had snatched this beautiful Arabian from the Germans, who took him from the French; the French took him from the Arabs. He was a pure Arabian, brown in color with a light mane and tail.

I spent hours with these horses. I learned the smell of their breaths and the look of their dark blue irises in their eyes. I found if I put my fingers in the side of their grey velvet mouths there was a space without teeth. They had soft tongues, not even as rough as mine.

I could slide onto their backs from the side of a standing stall and just sit on them. They liked me. I draped forward to hug them and rub my face in their furry manes. Their smell filled me with happiness. I often told them stories about my parents, brothers and Lulu. I'd sit or stand in the deep wooden manger in front of a horse and talk to her. I'd talk about things I thought the horse might like to know. I'd look carefully into her eyes to discern if she understood. I was reassured by a nod. I was never kicked, bitten or stepped on.

Some had wonderful names: Joan Crawford, Blondie, Sapphire, Lady Sussex, Philomina, and Opal. There were several breeds: Shires, Percherons, Clydesdales and a Boulonnais.

After a few years, the horse enterprise ended. Canada was

exporting horse urine to the United States for fifty cents a gallon. We couldn't afford the workers, hay or feed, so we sold them except for a couple of riding horses.

Chapter Three

LULU

The years Lulu Taylor spent with our family

had the best effects on me. I grew to love her as much as I did my mother.

I AM BROWN

> I am brown because I am the darkest negro with coral
>   palms and foot soles.
> Brown Black of dark wet pine tree bark
> where souls of murdered slaves reside.
> Wet brown soft earth
> where creatures reside and play among themselves.
> Brown of my childhood placed upon me with clothes
>   I hated.
> Brown color now outside myself—calm, friendly
>   without internal placement.
> I am the darkest brown black of any African.
> I am loved by my Dah, my nanny, who never placed
>   brown clothes on me,
> but only waxed, starched pinafores—white, crisp and
>   sweet smelling.
> Brown left only—eyes and shoes.

I was in second grade when I went shopping with my mother. I pleaded for a pair of maroon, leather, buckled shoes. The golden, shiny brass buckles were set off to the sides. They could not get loose like my laced ones often did. I pranced around that night admiring them and thought about the next school day. How proud I was!

At school, several girls laughed and pointed at my shoes. "They's just like my daddy's. They're boys' shoes," they chided. As I looked down at my shoes, I suddenly hated them. I saw them to be ugly. Maybe they were like boys' shoes.

When I returned home I told my mother that my new shoes hurt and didn't fit. "They make my feet sore and I can't run," I complained. I showed her how I could hardly walk. I hobbled across the floor into the kitchen to prove my point.

Lulu told me to sit on the kitchen chair so she could look at my shoes. She took them off and asked me where the shoes hurt. I pointed to several spots. She removed my socks and looked carefully at my feet.

"They made fun of you at school, didn't they?" she asked.

I nodded in agreement.

"They're fine shoes," she said, "and you loved 'em before. Now you just pay 'em no mind. Those kids—you just pay 'em no mind."

I continued to wear my shoes to school because Lulu taught me how to deal with cruelty. I didn't have to heed others' criticisms.

Ever after, when someone criticizes me, I can imagine her saying, "Just pay 'em no mind." Lulu was a stable part of my early life. In retrospect, my parents were often oblivious.

I learned important beliefs about life from Lulu. She told me not to jump out of bed as soon as I woke up. She said it's important to let your spirit get back into your body because it travels at night. I think it might. Many years later I still don't jump out of bed as soon as I awake, but collect my thoughts first.

She advised me not to talk about bad dreams because you might make them come true. She cautioned me never to make fun of others. This is good advice. I have a story that proves what you do may become manifest. My brother, John walked into the kitchen one day mimicking a crippled man. He contorted his body, right arm and face to imitate a crippled man he had seen.

Lulu said, "Careful! Don't make fun of a cripple, you may mark your child."

Indeed, that is just what happened. My brother had a baby girl born with a withered arm. A band about the upper arm had to be cut to release the blood flow. She is an adult now with one arm and hand much smaller than the other.

I did fun things with Lulu. Every time we got a new dog, both of us would lard its feet, so it wouldn't run away. When I lived in New York, our puppy ran away. We didn't know it had run over the bridge to Brooklyn. The first thing I thought of was—I didn't lard his feet. When we got him back, I did lard him up, and guess what, he never ran away again!

Lulu was a no nonsense person. She had a quiet determination like a deep undercurrent, silent but ever present. Maybe people think Lulu's beliefs and mine, and more that I haven't written about, are superstitions, but there is power in beliefs.

Walter Hains, our outside man did something to Lulu that she immediately put a stop to. In summertime, Lulu liked to iron in her stocking feet while standing on newspaper. She said the paper cooled her feet. I was in the living room watching her iron in the kitchen. Walter came from behind her and pinched her backside. As he walked by her, he raised his right arm. Lulu calmly turned and pressed the iron onto it. Ouch! Nothing was said. I believe he never tried that again.

One summer night I thought I heard something and peered down at the yard from my window. I saw Lulu walking around the outside of the house—checking. She wore her black silk kimono with an embroidered dragon on the back. My brother who was in the navy, gave it to her when he returned from Japan. She stealth-ily walked so as not to awaken anyone. I saw she was smoking something larger than a Chesterfield cigarette. It was a cigar! I had never seen her smoking one because she always smoked cigarettes. I cherished the way she kept her secrets and I learned how to keep them too. It was nobodies' business if she smoked cigars and I kept that secret too, until now.

When I was about five, Walter died. He was probably in his seventies at the time. His sickness began with a fever and weeping sores that covered his entire body. My mother and Lulu cared for him by emptying his bedpan, washing and feeding him. I recall Dr. Boyer coming frequently to treat him at our home.

Once, I stood near the doorway to Walter's room trying to see what was going on. My mother scurried over and ordered me to immediately go upstairs. A peculiar smell of burnt rope permeated the cellar. Several days later Walter was buried from our house. He had no relatives, so my father bought a coffin and paid for his burial.

I tried to see him close up in the open coffin but I wasn't tall enough. My brother, Bob, held me up to touch Walter's cheek.

He said, "Don't be afraid, Walter is dead." Although he appeared so very still, I stuck out my finger and touched his cheek. Lulu took me to the sink and immediately washed my hands.

At the burial service, a minister came to the house and prayed by the coffin. My father, mother, brothers and Dr. Boyer stood quietly. I stood on a dining room chair at the back of the room to see while Lulu held my hand so I wouldn't fall. That was my first experience with death. Death meant something was very still and could never move again.

Chapter Four

SEPARATION

As a child I was often sent away or separated from the things and places I loved. This pattern continued into adulthood. When I was three, my parents left on a winter vacation. I stayed with a couple in High Bridge, New Jersey. The Ronics lived in a small old house near the railroad tracks. Blue rug patterned Congolium covered the floors. A lone blue chair sat in the living room near a kerosene heater. A plain wooden table and chairs all painted white stood in the small, chilly kitchen. My parents met the Ronics through Betty, their daughter, who was a local telephone operator. Mrs. Ronic was stout and loving. Her smile bared uneven, stained teeth. Mr. Ronic was a railroad worker. I don't remember what he looked like, but remember at breakfast he had me listen to Rice Crispy cereal for the first time. I heard the snap, crackle and pop as it took in the milk. Some years later, I learned Mr. Ronic hanged himself in their cellar. My father cut him down.

Later, when I was about seven, I was sent to Aunt Eliza and Uncle Alley Knapp. I was to stay at their large beach house in Peconic, Long Island for a couple of weeks while my parents vacationed. My brother John drove. The huge house and wrap-around porch faced the bay. It was built in the early 1900s. Large spacious bedrooms painted in pastel were named for colors: the peach room, the blue room, the yellow room and the green. I was assigned the peach room. Large windows with white organdy curtains overlooked the water.

My father's older sister and husband were from an older generation. They both were born in the 1880s. They were organized and reserved. I came from a life on the farm where I roamed with horses, walked barefoot in freshly plowed fields, and searched for abandoned kittens in the hayloft.

I was in a western phase, since I had recently met Roy Rogers, who kept his horses (two Triggers) in a nearby town, when he showed at Madison Square Garden. My parents were gone when I left for Long Island so I dressed as I wished.

I arrived in worn Acme cowboy boots, a red western shirt, and baggy blue jeans. I wore a new plastic glow-in-the-dark belt. It was opalescent with black western images of horse shoes stamped across it. If you took it into a dark room, it glowed like a pale green snake. It had been advertised on the radio, and I was a proud owner. My frizzy, permed hair flew wildly about my head. I brought shorts, T-shirts and a bathing suit with matching rubber swim shoes. After greeting me, I heard my Aunt Eliza say, "What have we here?"

The place seemed exciting. I had never been to Long Island before, or seen so much beach or water. John left after dinner and my aunt and uncle taught me how to play Canasta. That night in my spacious room, cool salt air wafted through the window. I peered at the strange and dark sky above the vast water. A small lamp made weird shadows on the high ceiling. I slept with anticipation of the next day.

I awoke to cool breezes and stirrings in the kitchen. Aunt Eliza was cooking a breakfast of cocoa and pancakes. We were going fishing for porgies and blowfish.

My uncle steered his medium-sized motorboat into the bay. We cut up frozen squid for bait. I caught several fish. Once out of water, their gasping and flopping made me upset and sad. I didn't want them to suffer. My uncle stabbed them in their heads with a big knife so they died quickly. He said they didn't suffer. I didn't like fishing.

My face and legs got sunburned to the color of a lobster and made me cranky. When my uncle docked the boat, concerned for my safety, he made me sit on a nearby piling. Hot, sticky creosote stuck to the back of my bare legs and burned. Back at the house, my aunt rubbed vinegar onto my sunburn with a penny. That was supposed to take away the horrible pain.

I learned how to fillet fish. Blowfish were easy to clean. My uncle cut out the meat on each side of their back. He later tacked their skins on the side of the house to dry and use later as sand paper. We had fish and coleslaw for dinner. Aunt Eliza made pie. Canasta was again on the evening agenda. I was not having a good time.

The next day it rained a soft rain. Aunt Eliza painted ceramic molds of hands and dishes to be fired in a kiln. She gave me a delicate model of a hand to paint. I wanted to make a present for my mother. I dipped lace in slip and attached it onto the wrist part. I painted the hand a pastel pink. I thought I was doing a good job. However, in the process, I managed to spill a bottle of pink paint three times. My aunt became angry at my clumsiness. I became morose because of her anger and the rain. I stood on the porch in the damp, windy air, lonely for home.

That evening, while mastering Canasta, I cried. Even though my uncle made jokes, I could not be happy. I wanted to leave. Two days later, my brother drove out to take me back home. The farm, even without my parents, was a happy place to be because Lulu was there.

When I was nine, my parents sent me to Camp Salvadale, in New Jersey. It was owned by two elderly women, who I think were in their seventies. One was my father's client.

The camp consisted of several cabins spread across a grassy lawn. Six girls and a counselor were assigned to each. A large wooden entrance building on a hill housed a basketball court. I thought camp was going to be fun. I wore new green shorts, a shiny, white T-shirt and new "PF" sneakers. My mother bought a yellow plastic rain coat for me just in case it rained. I was ready.

The cabins had spring beds with gray, woolen blankets. The beds stood on dusty, unfinished wooden floors. My cabin had a lone large dresser with a hinged mirror bracing the wall. I put my clothes in one drawer and put my suitcase under the bed. I found there wasn't much to do. We took hikes, which were really walks up a path near a stream. We lunched in the large building on bologna sandwiches, then napped before swim time. I wanted to swim. I had learned in the Mulhokaway creek, a large flow in back of our farm on Wescott's property. The camp owners didn't believe that I knew how to swim, so I spent swim time sitting on the bank watching the older girls and counselors swim.

Mornings, we sang "Yes Jesus Loves Me" in Chinese. One of the women owners had been a missionary in China. A rainy day came; we marched to the building with the basketball court. While sitting on the court in a circle, we threw a red rubber ball to each other.

At dinner, dessert was a two-inch section of cake my mother had baked. The cake was cut so everyone got a piece. It had been boxed and tied with string. I asked for the long string, which I placed around my neck. I would not take it off. I was homesick and felt betrayed. I realized my mother had brought the cake and did not see me. I felt abandoned and shocked that she did that.

I wore an inexpensive wristwatch with a plastic crystal that my father had given me. I obsessed with keeping it wound so it would not stop. Tending to the wristwatch and wearing the string from the cake were desperate attempts at not feeling separated from my mother and home.

The weekend came and my mother came to visit. I begged to go home to the farm. I pulled my mother away from the two owner-women who were vying for her attention. I showed her the string about my neck and was sad that she didn't see me when she brought the cake. I sobbed and told her that I didn't want my watch to run down, because she helped me set the time. I complained that I couldn't swim because the owners didn't believe I knew how, and that we only passed a ball around as we sat in a circle in the basketball court because we couldn't go out in the rain.

It worked. I went home to Lulu, the animals and freedom. Once again, I sat in a field waiting for groundhogs to come out of their holes, and searched for lost kittens in the hayloft. I would draw, color with paints and crayons, read, look for turtles and visit the chickens. On hot summer nights, my brother Bob and I would sleep outside on army cots under the stars to escape the heat.

After sixth grade, my mother decided I should go away to a Catholic boarding school. Mount St. Mary's Academy wasn't far. A friend's daughter attended. The school had grades eight through twelve. My mother wanted me to go and decided I could should skip 7th grade. She rushed to the academy and met with the mother superior to see if it was possible.

She returned with a pile of books for me to devour. My former fifth grade teacher, Sylvia Chayat, was hired to tutor me through the summer. I was tutored in a spare bedroom away from distractions. The chairs were hot and sticky. Mrs. Chayat came three times a week to teach me and review the homework I had completed.

The boxed math problems were impressive. The problems of how many nuns did such and such and how many other nuns did or didn't do this, provided questions for percentages or fractions. The math was daunting.

I wanted to be outside with the animals. I finished workbook after workbook. Mrs. Chayat wanted me to learn and I did.

Fall came and I was off to a new school and in 8th grade. I slept in a large open dorm. A nun slept there too, but she had curtains around her corner of the room. Boarders were monitored and never left alone. Time was broken into blocks of prayer and study. Students were allowed to go home every other weekend. That seemed a long time to me.

On Saturday morning, we laundered and ironed our clothes. My cotton slip had a rose transfer. Transfers were waxed designs on paper that could be ironed and transferred onto a fabric. Lulu and I had carefully placed the design down and ironed it, transferring red petals and green leaves onto my slip. I thought the flower was beautiful. The nun did not. She chastised me for having a design on my underclothes. The other students looked on with distain. I felt shamed and tainted. I sheepishly put the slip away in my dresser.

That entire week I could not and would not eat. The dining tables had bright yellow cloths. Each of us had brought a silver napkin ring engraved with our name. It was a required item. Mine was oval with block letters. I sat to eat, but was too lonely and sad. Nuns advanced and coaxed me to eat, but I couldn't choke down any food.

In retrospect, I don't know exactly why I couldn't eat. The Catholic school's critical, cold nuns were unloving and unfamiliar. I was separated from the farm and what I loved.

I lost ten pounds that week. My mother came to pick me up. I had failed her aspirations. But Lulu was glad I was home. We could play checkers or Pegity again. She promised to show me how to embroider napkins.

I entered a wonderful new school in Union Township, New Jersey which was about six miles from home. Summer tutoring and my hard work with Sylvia Chayat, my fifth grade teacher, gave me the opportunity to skip seventh grade. Yippee! I was in 8th grade. I was home and loved my country school amid grass, birds and fresh air.

Chapter Five

SICKNESS

My parents often argued at dinner, fighting over money my mother spent for the children's clothes and other needs. My mother defended herself for the spent money. I cried often. This angered my father more; he would say, "Look Jean, you're making the child cry." I tried never to cry at dinner. Arguing caused my mother to stop eating. "I'm too upset to eat," she'd say. She was thin and always weighed about a hundred pounds.

My mother left home frequently because of illness either to be hospitalized or on vacation. She had multiple abdominal exploratory operations to find the cause of her pain. The operations removed a gallbladder, appendix and uterus. Sometimes her abdomen was cut open so that the surgeon could look around inside. Sometimes she brought back intravenous tubing as a souvenir for me.

For years she suffered from ulcerative colitis. During those times, nurses came to the house to care for her in her bedroom. At one point her illness was so severe that a Catholic priest came and gave her the last rites. Generally, I was not permitted to see her, although she was upstairs in her bedroom. I was told that she might die. Throughout my childhood, I was afraid she might.

One time, I knew she was going somewhere when I saw Lulu, our housekeeper help her pack a suitcase.

I asked, "When are you leaving?" and although she spoke a time, I was too young to tell time. I felt a black, crinkly feeling of dread and despair.

She said, "I'll be back soon." But I did not want her to go. She was so beautiful. She walked slowly down the steps, through the living room and out through the back door. I watched her get into the car after holding onto her coat, trying to keep her from leaving, but to no avail. As the car started around the drive, I ran to the front living room window to grasp it with my eyes, as if by magic, hoping it would stop. It sped down past the cherry tree, disappearing at the bottom of the hill to reappear and then become invisible in the distance.

When she left for the hospital, I desperately tried to hold onto her presence. Once she was gone from the house, I wanted the clothes she had placed in my drawers left as she had placed them. I wanted to keep my shoes on, since she was the last to tie them. I wandered about the quiet house where she once was, finding things to make her still real. I looked at her perfume bottles displayed on her dresser. I searched a wastebasket and saw discarded hair from her comb and a tissue marked with lipstick when she had blotted her lips. Her room was so quiet.

When I was a little older, I wrote letters to God and burned them secretly in our sheep barn. These were pacts bargaining for my mother's health. I made a pact with Jesus. I found a small card with a picture of The Sacred Heart of Jesus. Jesus had golden rays exploding from a ruby, red heart on his chest. I was sure Jesus would cure my mother if I was really good and perfect. It seemed I was never perfect enough. Although she didn't die, she continued to get sick.

In my early years, when I was seven or eight years old, my mother believed I had poisons inside me. She gave me cathartics every month to get rid of the toxins. She gave me enemas a couple of times a week. As I lay on the bathroom floor, she insisted I stay still and not cry as she poured a soapy solution into my behind. I learned to be quiet. Rarely did I cry, even when I scraped my knees or fell down. Crying upset my parents and I needed to keep my tears inside my eyes.

I believe my mother thought poisons caused sickness. Our family became sick because dirt got down our drinking water well. I was five at the time and got a severe kidney infection and was hospitalized. Luckily there was a new drug called Penicillin. For two weeks, I was hospitalized in Easton Hospital in Easton, Pennsylvania. I was given painful injections in my behind two times a day. They were so painful, I cried when the nurse came to stick me with them. One nurse told me that if I didn't want the injection in my behind, she would stick it in my eye!

While I was hospitalized, my urine was collected to retrieve the drug so that it could be reprocessed. My parents were allowed to visit for only one hour in the afternoon. Once they brought me vanilla ice cream. I was in a children's ward where an older boy had burns from a gasoline fire. He must have been about 8 years old.

Each evening, tall nurse, Dolly, wheeled me down the hall to get me a Coca-Cola. When I returned home, I drank distilled water for several weeks to rest my kidneys.

One day, when I was about seven years old, I decided to operate on my dolls. These were my favorites, having delicate bisque faces, arms and legs. Curls of brown hair were fixed to their heads. Their blue eyes opened and closed but they had a flaw. Each had a porcelain cylinder inside her cotton-stuffed trunk that produced a doll-cry. A bellows sounded when the doll was moved about, "Aah Aah."

I carefully placed each on a small bench covered with a white pillow slip and operated like I imagined my mother had been cut open. Carefully, I cut them with a small scissors and removed the crying culprit. I patiently sewed them together and kissed them. Now they didn't have to cry again, only open and close their eyes.

Chapter Six

NINE YEARS OLD

In 1951, when I was nine, my parents made a trip to California. They wanted to visit my brother Tony who was in the Navy. The aircraft carrier Philippine Sea had come in to port at San Diego. We planned to visit the Stoeltings too. As I recall, I didn't think much about visiting them. In my mind, they were far away and I was excited about seeing the West.

We set out early on a starlit morning. Our large, gray second-hand Cadillac rumbled down the long dirt road to Route 22. We headed for Chicago to pick up Route 66. The car had scratchy seats that itched my legs if I wore a dress or shorts. This day, I dressed in jeans, and sported new cowboy boots, my trusty glow-in-the-dark plastic belt, and a plaid neckerchief (really my father's handker-chief). I was going out West!

I had a new pair of brown dress shoes that were loafers with a slightly raised heel. I kept them in the back of the car in their box. Periodically, I'd examine their newness and sniff the new leather. Wide black stitching made a design up the front. A saying written inside confounded me for years: "As We Sew, So You Reap." Only years later did I understand its meaning. I had new white, pressed socks with scalloped edges, and two new outfits. I brought several horse books and a worn Miller Stockman catalogue. Sepia pictures depicted wonderful basket-embossed saddles and stovetop boots. It offered grazing bits for horses and chaps for cowboys. I imagined how a horse of my own and I would look with any and all of the items, and had spent hours doing so. I had ridden my father's horse

Lady in the front corral, for supervised rides on a safe horse.

I also packed a square, hand-held game with numbers fixed within a frame. The square plastic numbers filled up the frame except for one space. You moved the numbers about till they were in sequence from the top left to the bottom right. After scrambling the numbers you repeated the game. I had a blanket and a pillow in the back for sleep, but I was too excited for that and strained to see what was whizzing by.

Lulu packed chicken sandwiches on buttered homemade, white bread. These had been carefully wrapped in wax paper and laid in a box along with apples, a knife and a tea towel. There was a gallon glass jug with water and a large, glass-lined black thermos with red and yellow stripes. It had an aluminum screw cup, and was filled with black coffee secured by a cork. We had drinking glasses, too, the kind served at soda fountains with a bulge near the top.

Sunshine blazed the way as we sped along. I imagined horses, Indians and cowboys, and canyons filled with more Indians and cowboys, cowgirls and cactus.

I heard about the West from my mother who had gone there, in the spring of 1946, with Hugh and Marj Kent. My mother had become exhausted caring for my father's elderly aunt who lived with us. She was ninety-eight and suffered from high blood pressure and frequent nose bleeds. After many days and nights without sleep, my mother became weak and depressed and subsequently dreamed of being run over by a freight train. Our family doctor, Dr. Boyer, prescribed a vacation.

She mentioned this to Hugh who suggested she tag along on their honeymoon. She wasn't sure. Hugh argued that Marj had never been away and might get homesick. Hugh Kent was a Texan who was once a reporter and editor for the World Telegram and Sun in New York. He left reporting and moved to New Jersey where he built the Barn Theater in Frenchtown, New Jersey, and married Marj, who sold theater tickets.

I listened to my mother's adventures as they drove to south Texas, where they fished catfish from the Rio Grande. They visited Nellie Bea Kent, Hugh's aunt, who never paid for a haircut if it didn't suit her.

Hugh's friend in Austin, Horace Saule, was nearly shot by his wife when he arrived home a night early. It seems his wife heard a prowler and saw a silhouetted person at the bottom of the stairs. As she aimed her six-shooter, Horace whistled. This small act saved his life.

After visiting in Austin, they drove to Juarez, Mexico to drink pulque. Hugh had too much and pinched a Mexican woman's behind as she walked by. Her boyfriend flashed a knife. None of the three spoke Spanish. My mother and Marj made frantic gesturers indicating Hugh was drunk; after apologies and my mother's attempt at speaking high school French for Spanish, they left without a stabbing. The next day, I was told, the three started out in silence. Finally, Hugh said, "I like the damn tolerance," and that broke the ice.

My mother raved about visiting the King Ranch where she saw a black Labrador climb a tree. Her many stories about her trip filled me with enthusiasm when we started out for the West Coast.

On our first day out, while attempting to eat the chicken sandwiches Lulu had made, we encountered a joke. Lulu inserted chicken leg bones and a wing bone inside the sandwiches.

When we reached Chicago, our old car broke down. My father learned it could not be repaired for several weeks, so we went to a Studebaker dealer. He haggled for a new car while my mother and I sat patiently nearby for what seemed hours. Finally money for our new Studebaker was transferred via Western Union. We drove off in a new light-green car with bomb-like headlights. Because the car's engine was not broken in, my father could not drive faster than

40 miles per hour. We crept along route 66 while my impatient father fixed his eyes on the speedometer.

After three days in the new car, he allowed my mother to drive with prompting.

"Yes, Tony, yes," my mother repeated.

Not only was she able to drive a car, but trucks and tractors. She had even flown a PT 19, a British plane used during WWII.

One service station rest room amazed me. My mother and I entered a large room with a concrete floor. In the center were three toilets in a semi-circle. An adult one and two smaller ones for children. I sat next to my mother. There was no privacy. It was the first and last time we sat together in this manner. Over the years, I've often wondered why anyone would have a strange array of toilets in an open room. Perhaps that was where the drain was.

My father hated to make rest stops for me or my mother. I had to pee and my father refused to stop.

My mother handed me a glass over the back seat and said, "Here, use this."

I filled the glass carefully, but had to pee more. My mother carefully emptied the glass out the window, ensuring she did not drop it, but this caused urine to spray back into the car on her and my father.

"Jesus Christ," my father said. "What in hell's going on?"

My mother explained I had to go more. We always stopped after that.

To me, my mother was beautiful. People thought she was a Powers Model. Even when traveling, she put her hair up in pin curls at night and wore smart cotton dresses and stockings in the day. She patted on Shalimar perfume and used Arid or Mum deodorant. She coordinated her clothes. Because of this, she had definite ideas of how I should dress. My constraints were relaxed on the trip. I was allowed to wear jeans during the day, but after we found lodging, I changed into a dress or skirt for dinner, even though we might be eating at a diner. As we traveled farther West, it delighted my mother to drink coffee at five cents a cup. We often ate at truck stops because the food was cheap and fresh.

As we sped into New Mexico, we stopped in Taos and stayed at the La Fonda Hotel. The dining room had white tablecloths and a high ceiling. My father bought a copper cowboy-hat key chain for me. I searched for Indians, but hadn't seen any. We were told the Indians stayed on the pueblo.

I wanted to stay at motels with pools, because I knew how to swim. Occasionally we found one with a pool and air conditioning. That was the best reward for sitting in the hot car all day. After two days in Taos, we headed to Gallup. The hot sun was setting as we approached the town. Dirt fields stretched out on the right and left. I spied my first Indian riding bareback. He wore a loose blue shirt cinched with a wide silver concho belt. We passed him. I was thrilled. I begged my father to stop, but he said we must find a nice vacant motel before dark. There wasn't one. We found a small dilapidated place offering a room for five dollars. It had a double bed, a metal fold-up bed with a lumpy mattress and a rickety small dresser.

When we first looked at the room, newspaper was spread on the bed and the dresser. The wooden structure had a linoleum floor and an adjoining small shower and toilet. My father searched the mattresses for bed bugs and slapped the sheets to see if they were used before and had been powdered. Satisfied, we stayed the night. The fierce heat lessened as the night progressed. A small whirring metal fan on the dresser circulated cool air.

We were cautioned to cross the desert at night. A couple of days later, we stayed at a wonderful motel with a swimming pool in Needles, California. The temperature was 110 degrees. We had air conditioning. My mother abandoned her stockings, and I wore shorts.

We made it to San Diego where it was cooler and stayed at another motel with a swimming pool.

The Philippine Sea aircraft carrier was huge, gray and depressing. The deck was so expansive, it was scary. As well as a plane runway, it was used as a football field. Sailors with white hats were hurrying back and forth on the deck. My brother explained that everyone was excited because Jayne Mansfield, the movie actress, had visited. She had left just before we arrived. My brother's cabin was tiny with only a small desk and bunk. There wasn't even a toilet or sink for washing.

After our visit with my brother, my parents and I crossed into Tijuana for a bullfight. Our tickets were for the shady side of the arena, but there was no shade. The wooden bleachers were hot like frying pans. My father placed a handkerchief knotted at each corner on his bald head for shade. People cheered to see the padded horses and picadors arrive. A fast little black bull emerged, followed by the matador. The crowd cheered wildly. The excitement turned to a gasp, when the visiting Spanish matador was gored in the leg. Blood spurted out as they carried him to the edge of the arena, while clowns in barrels and horsemen distracted the bull. The matador waved to the screaming crowd. Fans screamed unintelligibly. My father turned pale and began to slump forward. My mother yelled into his ear above the noise. She grabbed his shoulder, "Wake up! How can you faint? It's him or the bull." I was glad to hear the bull went free. After my father recovered, we shopped for carved leather belts with silver buckles. I got a new, sweet-smelling leather belt and a red leather coin purse.

San Diego and the bullfight behind us, we drove to the Stoeltings for a short stay. Tall redwood trees flanked the two-story house and swimming pool. Georgie showed me a tarantula in their garage. I had never seen one and was frightened. She didn't kill it, but poked it with a broom; it jumped straight up. She cautioned that tarantulas were poisonous. Now I know they're not. The house had a bar on the first floor with high stools. We ate dinner there. I remember many bottles of liquor behind the counter. I could hear Stoelting's low voice amid the smells of cigarettes, liquor and my mother's perfume as I sat in the living room. I remembered his words, "Little girls lie." I was so afraid of him, even though my parents thought he was wonderful.

I slept in a room with Georgie's mother. She suffered from breast cancer. Stoelting made faces at her behind her back, and referred to her as "the old lady." My parents didn't care that he did that. They were aware, but didn't pay attention. I went to bed early while my parents talked late into the night with the doctor and his wife about mining. Nothing bad happened to me that night. We left the next day for the Grand Canyon before returning to the farm. My father said, "Dr. Stoelting is going to make us rich."

It was a couple of years earlier, when my mother was well, that she learned to fly an airplane. My father had incorporated a nearby airport. My mother became enamored by flying after meeting Charles Lindbergh and his wife Anne during the Lindbergh-Hauptmann trial. My father traded payment for his legal services for my mother's flying lessons. I remember going to Fritchie's airport and waiting with the pilot's children while my mother went up. She wore a leather hat and goggles.

Sometimes she flew over the farm. My brothers and I would run out to the field and wave our arms above our heads for her to see us. She'd tip her wings at us to say, 'hello'. She wanted a plane of her own, but my father reneged. He was concerned for her safety because she had what the doctor called 'heart spells' which affected her breathing. That nixed an airplane for her.

When I was ten, my father gave me a wonderful retired Army horse. My father bought Sonny from an elderly woman in Clinton for fifty dollars. He became my escape and companion. I loved him. I first saw him the summer of 1952, when I was ten. He was trucked by Ted S. a horse dealer from Asbury, New Jersey, a nearby town. Watching from the porch of the farm house, I saw Ted's big red truck labor up the steep hill. Inside was a tall bay gelding wide eyed and snorting. He turned inside the truck with Ted's prompting and carefully walked out down the ramp. I was given the lead rope. He was mine! I checked him out and gazed into his beautiful eyes. He had a neck brand: 4T72–S. I thought the "S" meant he was sold or discharged from the army. It was as if we had met before. I loved him immediately.

My father bought an old wooden two wheeled horse trailer to truck him. The trailer could be drawn by our jeep that we used to pull the hay wagon. I wanted to go to the local horse shows like Donna B. a classmate. She had a small buckskin horse called Little Buck. If she tickled his back, behind the saddle, he bucked or crow-hopped.

Riding Sonny was great fun. I rode him over the pastures and along the fences. I pretended I was a cowgirl riding to check for stranded cows.

I competed in local horse shows and got some ribbons. I never won a "blue" because Sonny wouldn't change leads when he cantered. He wanted to lead with his left front foot when he cantered to the right. It didn't bother me because I imagined he tried. Besides, I was left-handed. I took good care of him. I sent away for a lined, blue duck blanket to keep him warm in winter even though he had a furry winter coat from being in the field. One Christmas, I bought a new, black halter at the local GLF feed store, which I boxed and wrapped. Christmas morning, I ran to the barn to show him his present. I took off his old halter and carefully buckled on the new one. I was sure he liked it. He often nickered, when I approached, and pawed the ground as if to say, "Let's go!"

Chapter Seven

ELEVEN YEARS OLD

Dr. Thomas Stoelting made many trips

back East to stay at our farm. Except for the first time, he came alone. I will call him Stoelting because his last name reflects his personality more than the benign name "Thomas." He dressed in khaki pants and shirts, and Clark's desert boots. A cutout silver "S" on his belt buckle suggested a wrathful snake. In cold weather, when he went outside, he crossed a white silk scarf at his neck. He called it an ascot.

He smoked several pipes; some had fine, hinged, leather-covered cases lined with dark-green velvet. But the one he smoked most was a short pipe, with a pigskin-covered bowl with white stitching up the sides. He clenched this at the left of his mouth while supporting it with his left hand. While holding the pipe in this manner, he talked out of the right side of his mouth and could write with his right hand.

He often smoked Canadian cigarettes called Craven A's. These were packaged in flat red boxes labeled in bold-black letters. His German accent was thick and guttural. He claimed he could not pronounce particular English words, such as electric stove, or Elizabeth, but that was for attention.

He was in his fifties, about five feet six. His short neck and head topped a barrel-chest. Yellow front teeth shoveled slightly toward the back of his mouth. Gold-rimmed, nearsighted glasses added a calculated look to his menacing icy blue eyes. He doused his thick black hair with Eau de Pinaude. He shook generous amounts of "4711" toilet water onto a white handkerchief which he stuffed into his right back pocket, making sure a little stuck out so he could easily extract it.

One evening after dinner, my parents and I were sitting with Stoelting at the dining table. Lulu had finished cleaning the kitchen and retired to her quarters downstairs. Stoelting sipped coffee, drew on his pipe and began speaking in a soft mysterious voice. After clearing his throat, he motioned us to bring our chairs closer. He was about to tell us something special.

"In 1948 I was hiking in the hills of northern California near a place called Mountain Home looking for ore. I saw a flying saucer ship crash. It came over the hill flying slowly and low. It was silver and silent. Then it crashed onto the hill, scraping along the ground before coming to a stop. Presently a hatch door opened. Four short, two legged, pale-green creatures emerged. They appeared strangely human and without clothes. They had pointed ears and large green eyes. I can't tell you more, because I swore not to talk about the incident," he said. "I have connections with the government," he added, alluding that he had friends who worked in Washington, D.C. and had something to do with this.

He told us not to tell anyone about it.

My parents didn't ask questions. My father said, "Interesting." I believed it. I never heard of anything like this before. I asked Stoelting if they were from another planet and he nodded.

Stoelting often told one of us a secret, just for us, then tell us not to tell another family member. Months later he told me about a strange animal somewhat like a horse but smaller that lived on a planet where he came from. That was a secret for me. At the time I didn't know what to believe. I wanted to know just what this animal ate and what else was there, but he said the time wasn't right yet.

My father did buy a telescope at Stoelting's request, so we could view the night sky. Stoelting said outer space people lived on the moon and Venus.

Stoelting, my mother and I drove out on a lonely dirt road on winter nights to view the stars and moon through the new telescope. I wanted to know where on the moon the outer space people lived. I wanted to see them! Stoelting said they lived on the dark side of the moon. He said the "good" aliens lived underground on Venus and resembled humans. He warned us about the "gray ones," who were evil. Many had come to earth to make harm. They were from Mars. I wanted to know what harm they did, and how I could tell who was bad. "They're too bad to talk about," he said. That was all he said, leaving my imagination to conjure up what might be bad.

He showed us the moon's Mount Pico and craters. He said he was showing us these things for our future. He couldn't divulge why because it was a government outer space project.

Stoelting controlled our family by dividing us with secrets and at the same time telling us we were chosen for an important project. He schemed and set up a sexual affair between my father and his secretary. By imparting so-called secret knowledge, he made us feel special.

My family craved his presence. My mother adored him. She knitted socks and sweaters for him, and hats and mittens for his family left in Boulder Creek, California.

My father supported him because he believed that a mine's mother lode was going to make us all rich. In 1952, when I turned eleven, my father had been supporting Stoelting's mining ventures and his family for three years.

Our housekeeper, Lulu would not say she liked him. Stoelting would sneak into the kitchen wearing his soft-soled desert boots and try to scare her.

"Lulu, what goodies are for dinner tonight?" he'd ask.

"You have to ask the Missis," she'd say while rolling her eyes. She knew what was planned for dinner but she didn't want him nosing around in the kitchen. That was her domain. She sensed his intent to harm.

A family friend, Frances Decleene, said she didn't like him because he had a short neck. She was Czechoslovakian. She told my parents that in her country when someone had a neck like Stoelting's, he was the Devil. She believed when the Devil first emerged from inside the earth; people stomping on his head made his neck thick and short. My father, being a lawyer, didn't think that was relevant and I would agree, but it's interesting folklore.

My oldest brother, Tony, worshiped Stoelting. After graduating from Dartmouth, he left that summer to stake mining claims in California for him. At that time, my brother didn't know anything about mining. He had received a degree in English. He too, was excited about the prospect of getting rich. There was nothing my brother wouldn't do for Stoelting. It was hero-worship.

I was beginning to develop into a young girl. Although I had not had a period, my chest started filling out. Stoelting noticed. He teased me by calling me "Flea Bites," referring to my breasts. I was eleven years old. He told my mother I needed training bras.

Bob, my seventeen year old brother, rode along to Tepper's Department Store in Plainfield with me and my mother to shop for bras. Stoelting hurried to pick out Maiden Form training bras for me. They were made of elastic with cotton lace triangles on the front. He wiggled into the dressing room with me to check how they fit. My mother explained to the sales woman that he was a doctor. Bob remembers Stoelting stuffing a pair of woman's lacy underpants into his back pocket with the lace sticking out, then dancing about the lingerie department.

That evening Stoelting showed my parents a wonderful red light. It was infrared and made people's veins more visible. For my parents, this was a new wonder. My father took off his shirt and my mother took off her blouse. Stoelting showed them how their veins were revealed under the light. The red light was secret and special. Infrared lights were rare at the time.

Stoelting told them he had knowledge of the real effects of things such as this light. It was supposed to help my parents in something he alluded to but did not explain. Something important, perhaps they were going to a distant planet. He often spoke nebulously so others could fill in with their own aspirations. These were times when he spoke about traveling on spaceships. He claimed he was from Venus. He told how his outer space friends could hurt people and injure people's necks. He said this is what the grays, or evil ones do to others. Stoelting promised to show us more secrets similar to the light, but said he had to get permission first from those "higher up."

That same night, after the infrared light incident, Stoelting handed me a small bottle of some kind of oil with a peppermint smell. I was supposed to rub it on my breasts. He said he got it in New York and it was special. I used it once and was disgusted by the thought of him having anything to do with my breasts, and of putting this gunk on my body. Several days later, he asked me if I was using it. I lied and said I was. I was mortified and filled with dread and fear.

When Stoelting did this, I couldn't share my feelings with my mother, because she thought he was always right and because he was a doctor. I was unsure of how I should act. I couldn't do anything about my developing breasts, which weren't even there, and how Stoelting made fun of me for having them because they weren't developed. My parents heard him call me Flea Bites but said nothing in my defense.

One evening, after I was in bed, I called down to my mother who was in the living room with Stoelting. I wanted a kiss and to tell her goodnight. Stoelting ran up the stairs and bolted into my room in a furor.

"How dare you call your mother!" he yelled. "Shut up. Your

mother is busy listening to music and doesn't need to come here." I was shocked and terrified. I cried into my pillow until I fell asleep. He had removed my mother.

I was afraid of him and stayed away as best I could; I spent more time riding my horse, Sonny. I rode for at least an hour after school and more on weekends. I rode sometimes in a soft rain, over worn dirt roads to Wescott's adjacent property, then along the pasture fences and once or twice to the neighboring small towns of Milford and Frenchtown. My parents didn't mind because my horse was safe. I picked sassafras leaves to chew and sucked on honeysuckle flowers. I was content to ride in the country. My horse comforted me, because I whispered my problems to him. He seemed to understand. Now as an adult, I wonder why I did that, but I had been doing that kind of thing for years.

Chapter Eight

CHANGES
IN THE WEATHER

Over a period of years, from 1948 to 1955, Thomas Stoelting formed several mining corporations. Empire Exploration Corporation was formed for a uranium mine in Idaho. Prospective buyers were shown pictures of him and his partner Rolf Meuer working in western California, Nevada and Idaho. I remember some photos of the two camped in the snow in northern Idaho. Pictures of tents and equipment were intended to show to the stockholders how hard the two were working. They told how they staked mining claims. They said they staked a claim by placing a paper with the corporation's information in sealed coffee cans weighted by rocks.

When Stoelting was back East, there were stockholder's meetings at our house. Meuer stayed out west to continue staking claims and take ore samples for analysis. The meetings were peppered with Stoelting's bombastic talk about mining. He showed pictures and samples of ore. Greedy shareholders, smothered in smoke from Stoelting's pipe, filled our living room. Stoelting dressed in uniform-like khakis, a white silk scarf at his neck and desert boots. He reeked of Eau De Pinaud hair tonic and smoke. When a prospective stock-holder asked about the mining process, Stoelting replied defensively, "It's too hard to explain, there are so many steps in getting out the ore." He then shifted the subject, stating that any legal questions should be addressed to the counselor—meaning my father, the lawyer. I served coffee and cake my mother prepared. Some people traveled from Philadelphia to our rural area. Even a priest friend from Bayonne, New Jersey recommended the stock to his parishioners. It was word of mouth that brought many prospective buyers. The stock certificates were beautiful. They were engraved images of black, brown and gold swirls that surrounded an eagle with outstretched wings. Each was numbered in bold black letters.

There were setbacks for The Empire Exploration Corporation, and Stoelting had a story to explain each one. It would be bad weather in Idaho and flooding of the Snake or Salmon rivers. It could be waiting for the Security and Exchange Commission to approve something. The stockholders proved faithful.

My father was probably the largest investor because he bought stock and supported Stoelting's family still living in Boulder Creek, California. By 1955, my father had invested so much money in the mining venture, that we had to sell the farm. I was thirteen and in eighth grade.

I didn't want to leave the farm because it meant giving up my horse Sonny. After several weeks on the market, in the spring of 1955, our farm sold to Mr. and Mrs. K. a couple with a little girl.

Our new house on 56 West Main Street in Clinton was spacious having four bedrooms, two living rooms, a dining room, kitchen and summer kitchen. I was assigned a small bedroom that had served as a sewing room for the former owner. My mother was excited to decorate. She eyed heaps of wallpaper books before deciding to repeat the dusty rose color for the dining room. A large front room was saved for guests. My brother Tony, although away, got a large bedroom adjacent to mine. I got to pick the wallpaper for my room. I chose a dark green color because it reminded me of a forest in summer.

There was no place for Lulu, our housekeeper or Sonny. The K's little girl wanted Sonny. My father promised he would convert the garage at the new house into a barn, and buy me a new horse. Sonny was part of the farm sale. He was part of the deal. After I moved, I visited him once. His once slick coat had become dull and he was too fat. Not long after, my father told me Sonny had died of colic. The Ks. didn't know how to care for a horse.

Lulu went to work for Senator Bodine and his wife. Once my mother and I visited her after she left. She had become so thin. I thought, like me, she was unhappy. We soon lost contact because of my future problems.

Chapter Nine

THE SUMMER AND FALL OF 1955

Zippers

I loathe the sound of zippers.
Zippers open the fly for rape,

Zippers at mouth to keep quiet,
For eyes not to see.

The dreaded zipper of forceful sex,
With fear and terror,

And smells of Clorox and,
Blooming chestnut trees,

And Eau De Pinaud hair balm,
And mustache wax,
Over a German accent.

After I graduated from eighth grade, my parents and I drove to Denver, Colorado. My oldest brother was attending a school nearby. I wanted to go out west again. Before we left, my father hired Willie Augstein, a German man, who lived next door, to convert the garage. It would be a barn for my future horse. He would also build a small adjoining corral. The barn was supposed to be finished by the time we returned.

On the way, we stopped at Howard Johnson's restaurants to eat and Travel Lodges to sleep. Once we arrived, I visited the Miller Stockman Store. The rows of western hats and saddles thrilled me. The smell of shiny, new, leather saddles gave me goose bumps.

At the roadside, from Denver to Golden, horses were available for rent. Sunny Wabschall, who I believe was a Native American, rented safe ones. My father rented a horse for me while he and my mother visited my brother. For several days, I rode many hours over a nearby area and up to Table Top Mountain. I discovered an abandoned rodeo arena and watched bull snakes slither through high grasses. I loved being out west. My favorite horse was Foxie, she was small and sure-footed. Sunny, her owner said that she trusted me not to run her or get her overheated. I was just glad to ride slowly and take in the newness of the terrain. It was my first time to see a bull snake!

After we returned home to New Jersey, my father bought me a little horse that resembled the horse I rode in Colorado. He was a little, red gelding. I named him Foxie.

Because the barn wasn't finished, I boarded Foxie in town with a farmer who lived on Leigh Street. After school, my mother drove me to him, so I could ride in a nearby field.

Stoelting was due to arrive in September. He never brought his wife after his first visit in 1949. Anxious stockholders wanted to know how the mining operation was progressing, and when they would make money from their investments.

The summer of 1955, I rode my horse down the streets and through the fields on the outskirts of Clinton. By October, the barn and corral would be finished. The work bench under a window facing the house was preserved. A large barrel for oats and space for hay bales made the barn functional, although water had to be carried from a tap outside the barn.

At the beginning of September, Stoelting arrived. He drove his large Packard, he called it Suzie, up the drive. It was the same car that had broken down in 1949 when we first came to know him. My parents were excited with anticipation. My mother bustled happily about the kitchen while my father helped him carry his belongings to the bedroom with twin beds, next to mine.

I watched as Stoelting put his papers into my brother's desk and placed several pipes on the bookshelf. He placed his gun and holster on the dresser along with Eau de Pinaud hair dressing and 4711 cologne. My mother came into the room to help him unpack.

Cheerfulness filled the house because he had arrived. Stoelting wanted to know about my schooling and about my new horse. He wanted to meet our neighbor, Willie Augstein, who was also German. The elation of Stoelting's arrival continued with a large stockholder's meeting and several visits from Father Miller who recommended the stock to his parishioners. The thrill and delight continued nearly a week until my grandmother became ill and died from pneumonia.

My mother had gone to Plainfield to help her two sisters nurse her before she died. Her funeral was to be from the home. I traveled with my parents to help with the food my mother had prepared for the dinner scheduled after the funeral. Stoelting drove down in Suzie to document the funeral with his Stereo Realist camera.

The day of the funeral was cool and sunny. The large Victorian house shaded by tall pines showed impeccable care. Inside, shahrukh rugs, antique clocks and illuminated manuscripts behind glass created a solemn setting. My Nana lay inside an open coffin in the living room. The room was banked with flowers. Everyone talked in hushed tones to respect my dead grandmother.

After the interment, the family and close friends went back to the house to eat and drink, including the minister and undertaker.

People were happy that the funeral was over. There were so many dishes and pots to be cleaned, my parents decided to stay and help after the others departed. Stoelting said he would drive me home in order to give my parents more time to socialize and finish up.

I was happy to ride in the big car with leather seats. It was dark as we drove off. His car had a sun visor, wood paneling and a spotlight on the side. A green scent tree swayed from a long middle convex mirror. The heavy car lumbered along like a boat. I was tired and almost fell asleep as we approached the turn at Clinton Point Inn. Stoelting, whom I also called Dr. Tom, told me to sit closer to him. When I did sit in the middle, he put his hand up my dress, and pushing aside my underwear, put his finger inside me. I pushed his hand down and away.

"You should like that," he said.

"I don't like that," I said as I slid to the side. I cried.

"Stop it! Right Now! Stop baby crying! I care about you, and something is wrong with you if you don't like that. I have to cure you." He spoke angrily to me.

Again, he took his hand off the wheel, grabbed at me, running his hand up my leg under my dress, trying to put his fingers inside me. He poked my leg with his fingers. "You're hurting me, please stop," I begged.

"That's enough for now," he said, as he took his hand away.

When we parked at the top of our drive, I bolted, trying to get out the door. I began to throw up. Stoelting quickly gripped my shoulder and stopped me from escaping.

"You listen to me, Sandy. You do as I say, or you'll get it in the neck."

He said people who were hurt by aliens, "They got it in the neck."

I got out while he took his camera bag from the back. He told me to walk slowly to the house.

Stupefied, I walked up the stairs, dressed for bed, and shut my door. It had no lock. Stoelting opened my door quietly and stood in the doorway. He was dressed in a T-shirt and cotton Jockey underwear. He beckoned me by waving his arm. I shook my head "no," but he stepped forward and grabbed my wrist, leading me to his bedroom.

"You better be quiet," he said in his strange accent.

He then pushed me down on his bed and pinned me with his left arm at my shoulder and chest. As he did this, he pulled himself out from his underwear and pressed his penis inside me. I was horrified at what might happen. His cologne, T-shirt against my face and the strange pain I was feeling in my vagina terrified me. It was the most awful feeling and fear in the world.

In my mind's eye, I found myself suddenly at the doorway observing what he was doing to me on the bed. At the same time, I was aware of him on top of me and the terrible pressure of his arm and body. His penis felt board-like. I felt inside out and hyper-aware of the smell of his cologne and cigarette breath. Because I was aware from the doorway at the same time, I observed seeing his body over me in his cotton underwear. This happened quickly, but time slowed like a slow motion film. It was strange, because I was both under him and at the doorway seeing what he was doing. It was as if there were two of me or one of me in two places.

At last he stopped. A smell of Clorox wafted in the air and in me, which I later learned was the smell of semen. I was numbed. I couldn't feel anything. I felt like I had no body and did not exist at all.

Stoelting said, "Don't you realize this is for your own good?" He put his face to mine, speaking through his clenched teeth.

"Listen to me: If you say anything to anyone, you will force me to hurt your parents. You wouldn't want that, would you?" I shook my head.

I could smell the Clorox odor. The white easy chair in the corner was covered with his shirt and pants. He still wore his socks. I sat on the side of the bed in a daze. I was no longer present by the door as I had found myself earlier.

"Something is not right with you, and I have to cure you," he repeated in his thick accent.

I went to my room. Stoelting followed me to the doorway.

"You better not say anything, or you'll get it in the neck, and I will hurt your parents." He left, mumbling something I couldn't understand.

In the bathroom, the horrible smell of him was everywhere, although the room itself seemed the same. There were the same maroon towels and gray walls. While I brushed my teeth again, my face in the mirror seemed the same. It was not a dream. Something strange and awful had happened. Was something wrong with me? I tiptoed back through my parents' bedroom, through the adjoining door to my bedroom.

The covers of the bed felt cold and damp as I extended my feet. I cried into my pillow so Stoelting wouldn't hear. I was changed and fearful about what it all meant.

I heard a car on the gravel driveway and car doors shut. My parents were home. I stayed in bed and heard Stoelting pad down the stairs to meet them.

The next day brought rain. If there was school, I didn't go. My mother sat in the kitchen clutching a handkerchief. She wore a new black cotton dress, different from the one she had worn to the funeral.

"I'm going to wear black for a year," she whispered, "out of respect."

She rose and put bread into the toaster for me. I noticed her puffy eyes and wry smile as she poured coffee. I hugged her. I couldn't speak to tell her what happened the night before. She was so sad because of her mother's death. I feared Stoelting would hurt my parents and me.

I must have been pale, because my mother told me to stay home from school.

"You must be sad at Nana's death. You're so peaked."

The toast stuck in my throat.

My father was in the dining room finishing his breakfast. How could I tell him? Stoelting was still upstairs.

I could not concentrate. I did not go to my bedroom because of its closeness to Stoelting's. Instead, I sat in the living room and looked at magazines—flipping through the pages. The house was sickening and weird. The living room air, moist from the rain, made my body sticky. I tried to focus on the magazine pictures, but I could not. All the talk of outer space and Stoelting's threats about hurting my parents were a horrible nightmare. I was cloaked in fear.

Stoelting's words echoed in my brain: "Something is wrong with you and I have to cure you. You don't want me to hurt your parents do you?"

Words repeated in my mind like, "One, one, one," or "Even, even, even." Words or numbers with no sense just repeated. I believed I was crazy. If I listened carefully, I heard a buzzing in my ears.

I had to pretend nothing had happened, but I couldn't get Stoelting's smell out of my nose or mind. I cringed at the thought that liquid was inside me from his penis. I was contaminated. I froze as Stoelting came down the steps. My father had left for work.

I heard Stoelting's low voice in the kitchen. I arose and listened near the doorway.

"I'm worried about Sandy. She's losing her equilibrium," I

heard him say. What did that mean? I entered the kitchen to see him sitting close to my mother, his head near hers. Setting his jaw with a contemptuous smile, he glared at me, as if throwing darts from his eyes.

I did want to tell my mother what Stoelting had done. She had a look of bravery, as she often had in the past, when she left for the hospital. It was really a look of resignation. She smiled at me and nodded. I left the two of them talking.

I lay on my bed listening to the rain, searching the four corners of the ceiling. One, two, three, four, I thought over and over as my eyes went around. It was calming and thoughtless.

I thought, if I could move away, things would be okay; I have to hold myself together. Amid my quiet longing there was a blanket of dread. I was missing something. Part of my spirit was gone. Stoelting had taken it and messed it up. It was not within me.

I likened myself to a pie that had a piece missing, or a flower with its center cut out or petals that someone had torn off.

Nothing happened for a few days. I ate, went to school and rode my horse and acted normal. Stoelting didn't refer to what happened either. It had all gone away.

That weekend, I was at my small desk doing homework, when he knocked at my bedroom door and walked in. He didn't look threatening.

He smiled and said, "Your mother went shopping. Now you need to come with me. Come." He took hold of my wrist as I turned to get a better look at him.

"You have to be cured." He led me into his bedroom.

"Take off your pants."

I stepped out of my jeans and underwear. "Sit here," he said as he motioned toward his bed for me to sit on the side. He knelt down, spread my legs and put his face to me. His mustache scrapped against my private parts, as he made a horrible sucking sound. He got up and asked, "Did you like that?"

"No!" I said.

"You see, something is wrong with you, you should like that."

Crying, I grabbed my clothes and raced to my room. I was terrified.

In a short while, he came into my room smoking his pipe. He sat on the side of my bed for a moment before speaking quietly.

"You must not tell your mother about this, she is too upset. She needs you to be strong. You know I can hurt her. I have ways. You must be cured of your dread of sex, and I know what you need. Do you understand? Look at me! Answer me."

He got up, grabbed my chin and pressed his face to mine and looked into my eyes. I couldn't move.

"Yes," I said. I didn't know if something was wrong with me or not. He was supposed to be a doctor. My parents asked him for all kinds of advice and information and I was told to call him Dr. Tom.

Now, regularly, he began to have sex with me and "eat me" as he called it. When my mother was absent shopping and my father was at work. Time after time, he did what he chose. He was ever alert when my mother left. I strived to be out of the house when my mother wasn't home.

Something strange happened when he was abusing me: I was somewhere else, away from him looking on from the doorway or up near the ceiling looking down as an observer, yet still aware of his actions. This transition made me a zombie. Eventually my experience of being in another place stopped permanently. It left and when I tried extremely hard to visualize the Virgin Mary and ask her for help.

However, my thoughts were always dazed and heavy. I had a difficult time trying to think or study.

Stoelting sometimes gave me shiny blue pills he said were vitamins. He took them from a corked glass vial, which he stored in a leather valise. I don't remember feeling any different after I took them. At the time I believed that they were a type of vitamin.

I asked him about getting pregnant. He said, "I know when to use a rubber." Sometimes he did use a condom or withdrew, which left more of his Clorox smell all over my stomach.

He'd throw his large handkerchief at me and tell me, "Wipe yourself off!"

It smelled of his 4711 cologne.

I pretended I liked what he did, because once when he asked me if I liked what he did, I said, "No." and he became furious. He grabbed things from his desk and threw them to the floor and pounded his fist on the desktop and chair back.

One afternoon, I lay in my bed after Stoelting had forced me to have sex. I tried to figure how to get away from him. I curled up under the covers to comfort myself and keep warm. As I lay on my side, I studied the green wall paper. I had picked it out. I stared at it, carefully noting subtle overlays of white on a hunter green background. The square design gave me some joy, even though I hurt. My body felt as though it was layered with black lines from my front to my back. The feelings intertwined inside my stomach that I could not think about how I might defend myself. My privates felt shredded.

My mother came into my room to see what I was doing. I told her I was tired and wanted to sleep. I could easily fall asleep for an hour or two, because my brain was numb. I could hear Stoelting in the next room opening desk draws and crunching his chair against the wooden floor as he moved.

Eventually, I crept down the hall and into the bathroom to freshen up before going downstairs. I didn't want to see Stoelting more than necessary. If I was quiet, I thought I had some control.

I think one of the ways I survived being abused was that I focused on an object or objects in my surroundings. I concentrated on the four corners of the ceiling and looked from one corner to the next, round and round counting to the number four. Just looking at the corners, trying not to see or smell Stoelting's shoulder near my face. Then it would be over. I would pick myself up and leave in a daze. Counting the numbers one to four had a calming effect. I'm aware of the number four. I sometimes listen to my car cylinders running and hear the one, two, three, four repetition of the engine. Listening to it does not recall my abuse or conjure up bad memories. I'm sure that's because I had the number four in my brain before I was abused.

Sometimes Stoelting abused me several times a day. I became complacent and did what he wanted.

I wasn't doing well in school. My studies became harder. I had frequent headaches and stomachaches. I often went to the nurse and asked for my mother to pick me up. The nurse was frustrated by my frequent visits. I whined to her, and presently my mother came.

She still drove me to ride my horse after school. I was quiet at school and morose. I shunned classmates. I had no friends as I had in the eighth grade. At home, I spent time alone in my room, and spoke less at dinnertime. My father asked why I had been so quiet.

Stoelting answered, "It's puberty. You know, Tony, it's a stage."

The barn was finally finished. One afternoon I rushed up the hill to see how Foxie was doing.

Stoelting had taken over the workbench area with all sorts of equipment. He sat on a stool watching me as I entered. I glanced at my horse and saw he was fine. As I was leaving to go back to the house and change for riding, Stoelting grabbed my arm. I did not want him to have intercourse with me. I wanted to change and ride. He pushed me down onto the hay bales near the door and put his hand over my mouth. From over his shoulder I saw Foxie watching. He nickered. I believed my horse knew just how evil Stoelting was.

Again, as Stoelting zipped up his pants, he threatened me with the same fearful words of hurt as he did each time. I despised him. Any kind feelings I ever had previously were erased by hurt and the awful dread of what he called sex. There was nothing pleasant about it at all. Yet, I pretended by saying, "Oh yes it was very nice." Alone in bed, I cried silently most nights, not knowing what I could do. It was just how my life was.

When I went back to the house, I was undecided, to stay there or to go back and ride. I changed into jeans and went back to the barn. Stoelting was sitting on the stool tinkering with some equipment. I saddled my horse and rushed out the swinging doors. Stoelting laughed as I opened them. I supposed it was because I was trying to rush out and away from him.

The sun would be setting soon. I wanted to ride longer and to ride back in time to the happy days of my life on the farm where I didn't have to keep secrets. I had a lot to do. Cleaning the stall, hauling water, homework and making sure I acted as if everything was fine.

My report card went from A's to C's. I couldn't concentrate. My mother consulted Stoelting about my marks. He told her it was all part of growing up.

Because my marks weren't getting any better, my mother took me to my aunt's in Plainfield to be tutored in math. Stoelting came along and said he wanted my mother to buy me something at Teppers Department Store. He ushered us to the lingerie department. He picked out a white nylon nightgown and duster with a blue ribbon tie at the neck. My mother bought it for me. Stoelting whispered to me that it was for our wedding. My mother thought

I should adore it. She said, "Dr. Tom has such good taste." It was carefully folded in a box and put into a large shopping bag with red and green dots and with twisted, red, paper handles. My mother thought it was a good reward for the time I had spent being tutored. When home, I hid it under my bed toward the far wall. I didn't want it.

I was forced to wear it one day when I was home with a fever and a cold. My mother had gone to her dentist, Dr. Turner, in Somerville. My room was chilly and damp. I wore a brown knitted beanie to keep my head warm, and flannel pajamas.

Stoelting came in and asked, "Where is the nightgown I bought you?" I motioned under the bed. "Get it."

I jumped up and got it out of the box. He told me to put it on. He watched, as I did, then beckoned me to his room. When he was on top of me, he stopped and said, "You act like a piece of wood, you are not fixed yet. It may take a long time. This white gown means we are married. I want you to say you like it. Do you understand."

"Yes," I said.

He instructed me to fold the gown carefully back into the box. He watched as I did. I put the box under my bed, and I never wore it again. It stayed there for more than a year.

Stoelting started to make trips to New York for so-called treatments. My mother would pick him up at the bus station. When he returned he reeked of the smell of Iodoform which is an iodine like substance. He said he was getting treatments because of some problem from traveling from outer space. It was something secret.

During the winter, I participated less and less with my parents and at school. No one noticed. I had acted differently for so long, I was considered normal. One day was nearly the same as another. I had no friends. I don't remember much about what I did with my time. Obviously I couldn't study well. I didn't go to movies.

I continued to serve coffee and cake to the stockholders at the meetings.

I was instructed on weekends to cook eggs for Stoelting and make coffee with cream. I carried this to his room on a tray along with a cup of black coffee for my mother. She would be sitting on the side of his bed, calling him, "Thomas Titamous," in a flirtatious way. She'd laugh, and tell him about the next pair of socks or sweater she was knitting for him or his children. She had knitted extra thick boot socks for his treks in the mountains. It's possible that she was having sex with him during this time. I have no proof, but her future actions would beg the question–did she?

When not out riding, I stayed in the house listening to talk of mining ventures and mysterious things that had happened to Stoelting. He claimed he knew people in the government that would help the mining company's success.

He wanted to meet Hilda S. one of my father's clients. My father said he thought it was curious that Stoelting wanted to speak with her alone, but assumed he wanted to converse with someone in German.

I was good at keeping the secret and a low profile. Over time it became even easier. I used my energy to cooperate with Stoelting moment by moment, to protect myself and my parents, but the stress was enormous.

He told a story how he purposely cut into a man's leg with a chain saw. He said he left him to die in the forest. He told this in front of me and my parents one night after dinner. They treated the story as if it were fictitious. He told me that during the war, he strapped a cage with a hungry rat over someone's eyes, so the rat would eat out their eyes. He said he had nailed a man's feet to the floor in Germany. I heard stories of how he poisoned people with arsenic and other drugs that seemed mysterious to me. He told me he could make me blind by sticking a long hat pin into my eyes.

"So you better be good." He cautioned, "I can hurt you by squeezing you with my fingers in your vagina and rectum and then you can't move around. You will never know such pain as this."

His threats and stories were unending. This talk of what he did in Germany made me later wonder if he was a Nazi war criminal.

I studied Stoelting's every gesture as a mental defense: how he held his pipe and squinted his cold, blue, icy eyes and how he twitched his waxed mustache. I was trying to figure out how to act. I was resigned that I couldn't do anything about him abusing me. My parents would take his word over mine. He was powerful. They savored his every word. My older brother and parents loved him.

One day in winter when I was in the barn with my horse. Stoelting called me over to the workbench. He had glued a pulverized black stone into a gold locket. He fastened its gold chain about my neck and told me I had to wear it for protection from the "grays," bad people from outer space. He never spoke directly, but alluded to some type of evil. He did this too, when speaking about the uranium mine and getting rich. He would speak of some mountain where he knew there was much uranium or mercury, but not say just where it was. Everything was so secret.

One day in 1956, and still a Freshman in high school, I was in the barn getting ready to ride my horse. Stoelting sat at the bench by the window, as he did often, and took a shiny silver identification bracelet from his pocket and jangled it.

"Look, this is something special for you." I took it and peered at its newness. It was strange. On the side, where my first name was inscribed, were four drilled holes that had been plugged with copper. "What's it for?" I asked.

"It's for your protection from the dark ones," Which is another name he called the outer space beings.

"I need to solder this on you so it doesn't come off," he said.

He showed me another bracelet that had plugged holes also. That one was for my older brother Tony. I held out my wrist for him to place the bracelet on me. He took a small piece of cardboard and shoved it under the clasp section. Next, after heating some solder, he dropped a blob of the silvery hot liquid on the closure to seal it. I didn't know what to think about its powers. I thought this thing would be on my wrist forever and that I would never get it off.

I trotted down to the house and showed it to my mother, who was in the kitchen fixing dinner.

She glanced at it, "That's nice dear."

I showed her the side with the copper plugs, and asked, "What do you think it's for?"

"I don't know," she replied, as if she wanted to be left alone.

"Well, Dr. Tom made one for Tony too," I said. "I saw it. It's supposed to be for protection."

"Is it?" She asked, as she continued preparing food.

I expected her to know something, but she was too busy making dinner. She was still wearing black as she had promised.

The locket and bracelet made me believe I needed them for protection. At school, however, I couldn't take the bracelet off for volley ball. The gym teacher wanted to know why the bracelet was soldered on. I told her that it was special and I didn't want to lose it. I played volley ball and field hockey while wearing the bracelet.

Wearing the locket and bracelet, plus the forced sex, gave me what I call the black crinkles–it was a dense, creeping blackness that affected my sight. The feeling changed my perception of light to a dull brownish yellow hue. Sometimes my dreams have this light, a yellow ochre color.

My father noticed again how silent I was. I told him that many things were on my mind with school and everything. He accepted that answer. I felt like I was becoming invisible.

In the spring of 1956, during my freshman year, I had symptoms of venereal disease or VD. I most likely had it since September. I had severe stomach cramps and a yellow discharge. My mother took me to the same doctor who treated me when I was eight years old – Dr. Hance in Easton, Pennsylvania. My mother told Stoelting about the infection. He told her that I had gonorrhea since I was eight. It had been encapsulated in my body. She believed him.

I don't know if my father was told. He might have been told that I had a kidney infection. He was not involved in private things like this.

Every week, my mother drove me to Dr. Hance's for testing and for deep injections of penicillin in wax. Hance's nurse judged me by shaking her head disgustedly each time I entered the examination room where a sample was taken by the doctor. I tried not to cry. Every week our car rolled up Route 22 to Easton, a long, dreary and often rainy drive. I dreaded the doctor visits.

The nurse ushered me into a small, cream-colored room with a 1930's movie look. There were metal instrument cabinets with glass doors and stainless lever handles. A cream-painted examination table with metal stirrups was the main piece of furniture. Dr. Hance took a sample with a small, flat, wire circle which was attached at the end of a metal rod. The sample was then rubbed onto a glass slide and washed with purple liquid before he flamed it over a Bunsen burner.

A peculiar vapor puffed from the heat. The smell of dread. Still infected, so I got another injection. They were so painful that it hurt for days when I sat.

Stoelting often came along for company, making sure I was "good." The three of us sat in the waiting room, while my mother knitted thick, wool boot socks or something else for Stoelting.

The waiting room's dark woodwork, dingy pull-chain lamps and a worn patterned rug gave the impression of the 1800's. A dark wooden window sill framed a depressing view of an adjacent brick building.

Later, the three of us sometimes stopped for soup. I was not allowed to talk. Stoelting talked about mining deals he made in Nevada or what equipment he needed for more exploration.

The two spoke how something was wrong with my body. My mother said it was strange that I was still testing positive for gonorrhea. Stoelting reaffirmed the gonorrhea infection had been encapsulated for so long, that it was difficult to cure. I saw my mother nod in agreement. I was pretty sure the infection was coming from Stoelting, but was afraid to tell her what he was doing. I knew he would harm her, as he said he would.

Dr. Hance and his nurse seemed to be the only ones who were upset at my infection besides myself. I felt more tainted than ever. I hated my body. When I went in for the nurse to give me the injections, my mother spoke to Dr. Hance alone. He never asked me if I had had intercourse or had a boy friend. My mother had told Dr. Hance she was sure the infection had been in my body for years. Dr. Stoelting knew about these kind of infections.

Chapter Ten

THE ARRIVAL OF ROLF MEUER

In March 1956, Stoelting's partner, Rolf
Meuer came east from Randsburg, California to help with company
business. He was a tall man of German descent in his 60's with black
hair, mustache and dark eyes. He smoked cigarettes and brought
his small Tippa portable typewriter to write reports and other
correspondence for Stoelting. Stoelting said Meuer had once been a
bodyguard for Gerald K. Smith, an anti Semitic leader in the 1940s.

Stoelting bragged that he and Meuer were like-minded,
meaning both had German heritage. Meuer was quick to do what
Stoelting bade him say or do because he too, expected to become
wealthy from the uranium mine.

Meuer had gold claims in northern California. These were not
connected with Stoelting or the Empire Exploration Corporation.
In retrospect, I believe Stoelting wanted to get his hands on these
claims for himself.

Meuer was assigned our guest bedroom at the front of the
house. It was spacious, furnished with a double bed, a chair, a small
desk and a blanket chest.

Meuer placed his typewriter on a small bench at the foot of
his bed. He got busy typing up reports Stoelting dictated.

He brought photographs taken in winter of himself and
Stoelting in Salmon, Idaho. The photographs showed tents set up
in the snow and he and Stoelting dressed in puffy Eddie Bauer down
coats—identical to those that had been worn by the climbers who
climbed to the top of Mount Everest. The stockholders eagerly

viewed the photographs and were reassured of their investment.

Meuer came to corroborate Stoelting's story about the mining venture. His talks would increase investments from the stockholders for purchasing equipment like Jeeps and boats. The boats were for navigating Idaho's Snake River, where Stoelting and Meuer intended to stake additional mining claims. Stoelting would use a good part of the stockholders' money for his and Meuer's salaries.

Meuer wore khaki pants and shirts mirroring Stoelting. He too, like Stoelting, had a gun which he concealed in a small antique desk near his dresser. Meuer was quiet and soft-spoken.

He talked to the stockholders about the time they staked claims in Idaho during the winter and answered questions calmly. The stockholders admired the photos of their snow camp and believed that the two were hard working.

More shares were sold and money kept flowing in. Stoelting bought two red Jeeps and two trailered aluminum boats with outboard motors.

Meuer traveled to Newark and Trenton, New Jersey to buy mining equipment: Geiger counters, an Esterline-Angus recorder, Brunton compasses and custom foam lined boxes. Most of these items were stored in our barn. Stoelting installed a ship-to-shore radio in our attic. He told my parents and me it was to communicate with aliens. He told Meuer it was to hear radio programs from California.

He coordinated having sex with me when Meuer was away and the house was empty. I was still being treated by Dr. Hance for the gonorrhea.

My recourse was to cry at night, when I was alone, so no one could suspect anything out of the ordinary. I imagined I had a guardian angel who helped me keep the secret. I could never visualize her with wings, nor could I envision her face. She was plump, kind, pale and pinkish in color. I desperately hoped she existed and I'd fall asleep trying to imagine just what she really looked like.

Sometimes, Rolf Meuer rode along to my doctor's visit with my mother and me instead of Stoelting. Marj Kent, a recent widow, would occasionally go along, too, for the ride to Easton, Pennsylvania. Marj and Meuer were told that I had a kidney infection.

Once, the four of us, Meuer, my mother, Marj and I went to Gettysburg, Pennsylvania, to visit the battleground. Meuer had read about the Civil War and wanted to see an actual site. Marj drove her new gray Buick which monitored a set speed. When she drove faster than fifty miles an hour, the car produced a terrible, shrill noise.

A short time after Meuer arrived, Stoelting traveled to New York three or more times a month to work on a secret outer space project. My parents and I were told it was important, and were told not to discuss it with Meuer, because he wasn't supposed to know. It was something big. Stoelting implied that it was a project to save the world. The catastrophe was to supposed happen on February sixth of the coming year. He spoke more about outer space and his real purpose. Whatever that was, we weren't clearly told, but our family was chosen to help him with this new important life saving project. My parents believed him. I didn't know what to believe.

There was a special plan for my father. Stoelting apparently told him he was supposed to have an affair with his secretary. I'll call her Janet. Janet had been adopted. Stoelting used this history to lay the foundation of her secret origin. She was really from Venus, but not even she knew that. Janet's top teeth shoveled back similarly to Stoelting's teeth. He told my father that she never imagined how special she was. My father was supposed to have sex, so he could experience intercourse with someone from outer space.

My mother discovered the affair when she listened in to a conversation between my father and Janet on our extension phone in the dining room. When she confronted my father, he told her why he was having an affair. My mother was supposed to understand, and embrace his new adventure. She didn't.

She became angry, sad and very religious. She obtained a key to the local Catholic church. She prayed, but she could not deter my father from seeing Janet. She worked in my father's law office.

My father began taking Janet to court when he was trying a case and to restaurants for lunch. Although she was married, my father visited her and her husband on weekends to swim in the couple's plastic-lined swimming pool. This infuriated my mother. Gossip in the small town fanned the fire in my mother's heart. She pleaded with me to chastise my father. I tried to dissuade him. My father explained that he wasn't always happy with my mother. He said she was critical of Janet's smoking, the plastic-heeled shoes she wore without stockings and the plastic-lined swimming pool.

He said, "Poor Janet, she was adopted and didn't know who her parents were."

Fights about Janet were ongoing. My mother said she looked like something that had crawled out from under a sidewalk.

My father defended his actions and Janet. "You just don't understand what's going on. There are things I can't talk about."

He alluded to a secret told to him by Stoelting. Something that my mother didn't know and he couldn't or wouldn't tell her. Day by day, a wedge between my parents got wider.

At dinnertime, when Stoelting or Meuer were present or at stockholders meetings, my parents showed no antagonism toward each other.

My mother, however, continued to knit clothing items for Stoelting, Meuer and Willie Augstein, the man who built the stable for my horse. She knitted like Madame Defarge. Her aluminum needles clicked and hesitated in rhythm to turn a row. She rounded a sock heel in an evening. Her clicking knitting needles made my father edgy. "Jean, for God's sake, I'm trying to read," he'd often say. He'd then hold up a book he'd been reading and shake it in front of her.

She pretended not to notice and continued click-clicking her needles. After that, my father would leave the room, in search of a quieter place to read.

I was still infected with gonorrhea. As time went on, when Stoelting forced me to have intercourse, I no longer found myself elsewhere as I did in the beginning. I made myself totally blank-minded and numb of any feeling. I lied and told him I enjoyed what he did and tried to act as if I did.

I often imagined a soft pink, woolly-like misty blanket covering me. This comforting mist enveloped me. I went to this pink-gray zone until he finished. Afterwards, a thick, dull black blanket of dread covered me—like a black, funeral door crepe.

I believed I would never be cured of the infection. I managed to pass my freshman high school year even though my marks were poor.

Stoelting stopped abusing me for some time and I tested clear for gonorrhea. I was happy without fear. I was free of Stoelting. I rode my horse that summer and listened to Meuer talk about his friend Della Ghirbrach, who lived in California, and also had gold claims. I competed in several horse shows and won a few ribbons and trophies. Ted Smith from Asbury trucked my horse, Foxie. My father went to the shows, but my mother never did. She was busy at home.

Late in the summer of 1956, I went target shooting with Sheriff Leigh, his daughter and Meuer. I shot my father's pistol with a round cylinder, and once with Meuer's gun, an Army type. The one he kept in his bedroom desk. The four of us shot bottles and cans for practice. Stoelting and Meuer thought it was good for me to learn how to shoot a gun in case I traveled out West. The two described huge rattlesnakes. One was able to stretch across the hood of a Jeep—ground to ground. They told stories about sidewinders and another kind of rattler called a Mojave green. No one had ever survived the green one's bite.

In late summer, my father and Stoelting traveled to Salmon, Idaho for a week exploring land suitable for mining. I spent more time with Meuer. He liked rocks and wanted to visit mines in New Jersey. I went with him to a slate mine in Bangor, and a franklinite mine in Franklin. Franklinite rocks are florescent. I found some that glowed green under Stoelting's Ultra Violet Light. I wasn't thrilled about seeing the slate mine and the slabs that were used for roofing.

Meuer gave me a book called *Thirty Years in The Golden North* by Jan Welzl. It was about a man who traveled across Europe in a pony cart. Meuer made a board for my horse ribbons to hang on the barn wall. This would make my horse happy. He could see the ribbons he helped the two of us to win.

Life was fine until the fall, when Stoelting sent Meuer to stay at the Robert Treat Hotel in Newark. He stayed at the hotel to pick up equipment that was soon to be delivered out of Port Newark. This gave Stoelting the opportunity to resume his abuse, and saying the same old things and threats.

"You're still not right and your mother thinks sex is good for you!" My mother! He had her approval, and she did know. Because several weeks earlier, she and I had a conversation in the kitchen about Stoelting. I told her what he was doing and how it all started on the night of Nana's funeral. I didn't mention his threats to harm her or my father. I asked her if she thought what Stoelting was doing was O.K. She said she thought he had stopped. She had evidently known about it for some time. I asked her about my gonorrhea infection and how I never got cured. I told her I thought I was getting re-infected from him. She said she thought it was possible for the infection to have stayed in my body since I was 8 years old. This is what Stoelting had told to her and me.

I asked, "Don't you remember what I told you in the bathroom when Dr. Tom and his wife first came to visit, and what they did to me in the upstairs bedroom?"

She said, "I never suspected anything. I never thought he would do anything to hurt you." She   clasped my hand, as we sat at the kitchen table, and squeezed it.

"I love you very much," she said.

"What are we going to do? I asked.

"I don't know. What's done is done. Let's see what happens," she answered. She had no answer. She wasn't upset. She frowned and looked at me with her sad eyes. I wanted her to love me and I wanted to do the right thing; then I thought, everything would be fine. She said she loved me. I was no happier by her words, but upset because she looked so sad. Maybe she did think that the infection was encapsulated. Maybe she thought what Stoelting did and continued doing was O.K. Was it?

She spoke of Stoelting as though he was always right. After our conversation, she still drank her morning coffee sitting on the side of his bed, while he breakfasted. My thoughts were jumbled. I tried not to think about Stoelting.

A new school year was starting. I was determined to excel and get good marks. I tried to be alert in class. I concentrated on my school work and spent as much time as possible with my horse, Foxie.

Several weeks later, I again visited Dr. Hance. The infection was back. I told Stoelting about it. He reiterated that it was encapsulated and that was why it was difficult to cure. I thought that might be true and it meant that I was cursed.

Dr. Hance treated me with a medication injection every week and added pills. The treatment made me nauseous and depressed. I spent time in bed and missed many days of school.

I remember crying often in school, apparently for nothing serious. My father, Meuer and family friends still thought I had some type of severe kidney ailment. The school requested a letter from a doctor stating why I was frequently absent. Dr. Hance wrote a letter, at my mother's request, stating that I was being treated for a kidney infection.

Stoelting suggested I should not continue attending school until the following year. After all, I had skipped seventh grade, so it really wouldn't matter. So I stayed out. I don't know what Stoelting had said to my father, but neither he nor my mother protested. Initially, I thought this might be a good thing. I wouldn't have to worry about studying and achieving good marks, and I could ride more often.

This was a perfect plan for Stoelting, because I was always at home. I was captured. I couldn't ride my horse, walk to town or go with my mother grocery shopping. If I was too sick to attend school, I was too sick to do much else. I couldn't go to church with my mother either. Once, when I went to Plainfield with my mother to visit my aunt, my mother told me to duck down when we drove through town, so people wouldn't see me.

Stoelting continued to have periodic sex with me until October. He began traveling, again back and forth to New York, to work on a secret project. Miraculously, he lost interest in me. I finally was cured, and had no discharge. At the time, I couldn't believe it. I feared the symptoms would return and stay as they had always done. I was really cured. Even though the infection was gone, I felt tainted, dirty and shamed.

Chapter Eleven

THE SADDLE-FALL 1956

When my father and Stoelting returned

from their short trip to Idaho, Stoelting said he had ordered a carved, silver-embellished saddle for me. He ordered it from Clyde Stone, a saddle maker in Salmon. Stone was well known for his intricate leather carvings. Stoelting told Meuer that I would be surprised by the silver trim. When Meuer told me that, I said I didn't want a silver embellished saddle. I wanted a plain one without carving. Meuer suggested I write to Mr. Stone and tell him.

After reviewing my Miller Stockman store catalogue, I decided on a Bowman tree. A Bowman saddle tree slopes down at the front sides. A saddle with a tree like this was often used by calf ropers because they could easily slide off their horse to tie up the calf.

I immediately sent a letter to Stone requesting a plain saddle with a Bowman tree to replace the one Stoelting had ordered. Since my horse's back was short, I wanted the saddle to have a short skirt. Mr. Stone wrote back stating that he had already made a carved bridle, but would make a plain saddle, as I had requested. Meuer and I were the only ones who knew about the change. Stoelting found out later.

Stoelting's secret project in New York was supposed to save the world. A young woman named Jan Sherwood was part of the plan. Her involvement with the project was a secret to be kept from Meuer. Later we learned that she had met Meuer and Stoelting several years earlier while singing in a California barroom. At that time, Miss Sherwood was an aspiring singer.

Stoelting brought her East to stay in a Forest Hills apartment in Long Island, where my father supported her. She was part of an outer space hoax to siphon additional money from my family.

The secret, Stoelting told my father, was that Miss Sherwood, like Janet, his secretary, was from Venus. Miss Sherwood was sent to earth to make a record. The money she would receive from her recordings would help her adjust to earth and help others who arrived from outer space. She needed to adjust to living on earth, so people wouldn't suspect her as an alien. She was one of a few, including Stoelting, who had arrived from Venus.

My father was an insider and believed this. He paid for her rent, clothing and interviews with recording studios. The project frequently took my father and Stoelting to New York and Long Island.

My father was excited by his new secret role, but Stoelting and he excluded my mother and me. My father began sleeping in one of the twin beds where Stoelting slept.

Meuer changed his bedroom too. He complained of traffic noise in the front bedroom. Route 22 was the main highway between New York and Pennsylvania. It ran in front of the house, straight through town. Trucks that sped over the concrete road throughout the night were ticketed by our next door neighbor, Police Chief Harry Snyder. He drove an old, black convertible because the town of Clinton couldn't afford a police car. Officer Snyder attached a siren and a red flasher on his. He waited in ambush. Speeding trucks and cars stopped by the officer's siren brought money for the town. The increased noise couldn't be avoided.

Because of this, Meuer switched rooms with me. He slept in my small bedroom next to Stoelting's. I slept in the front room. I was nearer to the bathroom and the front stairs, which were directly above the hall leading to the dining room. In daytime, I used my room and desk as usual, while Meuer continued to type reports and smoke in the front room.

Although I was cured, I was still stuck in the house. Willie Augstein, our neighbor cleaned my horse's stall. We had an Irish Setter, Penny. I spent time in the living room with her and listened to records and the radio. But I finally won the argument on getting out. I reasoned with my parents; since I was out of school for the year anyway, why shouldn't I be able to go out of the house, ride my horse and walk to town.

In the beginning of October, I stretched into my cobalt blue pullover and walked to the bridge in Clinton. I stood by the low stone wall topped with wide slabs of rock. My eyes followed the ripples of water dashing over the rocks. I sat on the cold wall; I dangled my feet, and peered down into the dark pools near the shore. Being out by the river seemed strange and new, like a house when one returns from a vacation. I stayed by the bridge until sunset. The warm sun on my chest and face had felt as if I was experiencing it for the first time. I sat looking about and waiting for something I couldn't express. I didn't walk over the bridge into the town because I was afraid of being judged by people I might meet. I felt guilty and ashamed because I wasn't attending school.

The past year had blanks. There had been no joy in my life. My father's affair had been ongoing. I had read some and spent time with my horse but I can't remember just how I had spent all that time. I had spoken minimally with Marj Kent, Willie Augstein, and Meuer when they were around. There hadn't been much to say. I'd no friends since eighth grade. Stoelting's control of my life and my ongoing infection had kept me occupied – my friends had disappeared. I had stopped riding my horse because I was out of school. I had kept to myself and had tried to avoid Stoelting. I became a peripheral member in the family because I was a teenager. The adults talked about adult things.

I was often treated as an afterthought, when someone remembered to include me. Our family did nothing together. No movies, no garden or animals to tend, no dinner guests dining as they had once, when we lived on the farm. People who came to the house now were stockholders. Our family focused on making money from a so called "mother lode."

I was leery of criticism, especially from Stoelting, so I spent most of my time alone. I knew little about items teens wore, or what they did. I listened to a classical music station, read some from a book entitled "First Violin" and pored over Miller Stockman catalogues.

My mother and I went several times to Plainfield, New Jersey to visit my Aunt Marion. These visits, too, were not the same. We didn't sit at her dining table drinking Constant Comment tea and eating crustless chicken sandwiches, as we did when my grandmother was alive. My mother went to beg for money. She wanted money to send to Stoelting's wife, Georgie, in California. Georgie secretly wrote to my mother, asking for money. Each week my mother sent part of her grocery money. The Stoelting's lived in a spacious house in Boulder Creek. Large redwood trees bordered their huge lawn and swimming pool. Still, Georgie requested money for different items, for the children's clothes or food.

My mother had a woman come weekly from the local reformatory to help her clean the house. Although our house on West Main Street was not as large as the one on the farm, it had four bedrooms and two living rooms. My mother couldn't stand dust. I think her cleaning was a diversion from my father's affair, and his exclusion of her by sleeping in another bedroom.

October 23, 1956 was my fifteenth birthday. Stoelting wanted to try out the new company boats on the Raritan River. Those were the boats that were bought for traveling up the Snake River in Idaho. I wanted to go along and see the trial run. Mr. Volpe, a stockholder, Meuer, Willie Augstein, Stoelting and I drove to the New Jersey side of the river.

It was a dreary, damp-coat day. I sat on a large rock near a shed and watched the men put out the boats from the double-decker trailer. The river was choppy. The men had no life preservers. The boat engines were revved up, and two light aluminum boats headed toward the middle of the river. Willie Augstein and Meuer were in one. Stoelting and Volpe operated the other. As Augstein's boat made a sharp turn in the rough water, he and Meuer flopped out into the cold river. Volpe quickly turned his boat around and caught the front rope of the one sinking. Augstein was holding onto the side of it to keep from drowning, while Meuer swam to the shore. Volpe caught Augstein and held him afloat while Stoelting steered his boat and the tethered one to shore.

The four men docked the two boats after turning over the flooded one. Meuer and Augstein stood on the bank, shivering and panting as if they couldn't breathe. Augstein shook his head and spoke excitedly in German to Stoelting. Stoelting then laughed, and said, "Hah-ha, Willie doesn't know how to swim, but he's in luck today." Stoelting acted as if he thought it was a big joke. The men loaded the boats quickly onto the trailer. We piled into the jeep to drive back to the house. I sat in the back seat with the two shivering, wet men.

That night, after dinner, Marj Kent, Augstein, Meuer, Stoelting and my parents sang happy birthday to me. Pecan pie was a stand-in for my birthday cake. Stoelting said the trial with the boats went well and joked about Augstein not being able to swim.

Sometime in November, my mother and I were told about Jan Sherwood, who had been living in Forest Hills. Stoelting told us she had come to earth from Venus and needed help from our family to adjust. Meuer was not privileged to know this, and we were sworn not to tell him.

Stoelting wanted my mother to go to Long Island to meet

the singer. She refused. She suspected it might not be safe, since my father and Stoelting had excluded her from this New York project until this time. Stoelting and my father often talked in hushed tones, and then stopped when my mother or I entered the room. They eyed each other as if to say, "We'll talk later."

We found out later that my brother Tony who had attended MIT to study geophysics, knew Miss Sherwood and had stayed in her apartment in Forest Hills. That was the result of a fight that had taken place in the summer between my mother and brother. My mother had become so angry, she told him not to stay in our house. So he, too, became an insider along with my father, believing Stoelting's story that Jan Sherwood was from Venus.

When Stoelting and my father invited my mother to go to Long Island, she was suspicious for another reason. Several days before the invitation, Stoelting gave her some blue shiny pills to take. They were supposed to be a type of energy vitamin. After she had taken the pills, I found her lying on a couch in our living room. She was pale and appeared dazed. She told me she had felt a constriction in her body that had started as a tight band at her feet then squeezed its way up to her head. After it had squeezed the top of her head, it left. The pills she took resembled pills Stoelting had once given to me. He told me at the time that they were vitamins.

When she was asked again to see Miss Sherwood, she said, "If you want this Jan to meet me, she can come here to the house." She did come after Christmas.

I tried to figure out what was true or untrue and to figure out what was important to believe: Stoelting's outer space claims about Jan Sherwood, Stoelting's demand that my mother go to Forest Hills, and the secret of how special we were to be chosen.

All of it was confusing. I still wore the bracelet that Stoelting soldered on my wrist. I couldn't take off. And I still wore the locket about my neck containing the glued ground up rock. Stoelting periodically checked to see if I wore them. I wanted to lose them, but I cautioned myself.

One evening, Stoelting brought out a box of sparkly, five-pointed star necklaces. They were for my parents and me. There was also one for my brother Tony, who was away. The clear pendants, on silver chains, were about an inch in diameter. Stoelting displayed them carefully, and asked for a drinking glass. He held a star, and used the point to etch a line across the glass. We were amazed. He told us they were special and from outer space. They sure looked special to us. He ceremoniously clasped them around each of our necks. He said they were for protection from evil outer space aliens. It was important for us to wear these now because Stoelting's special project made us vulnerable to danger.

Later, we discovered they were simple quartz stars. At first, we didn't know that quartz was harder than glass and could scratch it.

When my mother visited my father's law office, she noticed Janet wearing a star too. This infuriated my mother. She immediately took off her star and replaced it with a large four inch silver cross.

Fights over Janet escalated. My father frequently mentioned her specialness. My mother stayed hot angry. One evening she noticed my father's star on his dresser. In anger, she snatched it and flushed it down the toilet. She'd had enough of Janet and the outer space business. A fight over the star ensued. Anger between my parents could be cut with a cleaver.

My mother confided in Meuer, Marj Kent and Willie Augstein about my father's affair with Janet. They listened, but didn't say much, which was probably wise.

Marj Kent had her husband's cremation ashes and wanted them spread onto the ocean. Point Pleasant, off the Atlantic Ocean, was a few hours away. Hugh had been all over Europe as a war corre-spondent during WWI, and as a newspaper reporter in New York;

Marj wanted his ashes taken to the seashore and thrown onto the ocean, so he could travel in spirit. Both she and my mother agreed this was a good idea.

One cold, December day, in 1956, my father and Stoelting went to Marj's house and picked up the ashes, to supposedly take them to the New Jersey shore. I was walking on up the hill to the barn, when I saw the two standing at the top. My father took a box from his deep overcoat pocket. Stoelting said, "Just put them out here. It won't make any difference."

My father opened the box and dumped Hugh's ashes on the lawn, between the barn and the house. The gray-white powder dusted across the lawn like talcum. I wondered why didn't they take the ashes to the ocean as Marj had requested? I decided not to tell her or anyone else about it.

One night when Marj came to dinner my father told her, "The ashes are taken care of."

"Good." She said.

Since the ashes had been scattered on the lawn, I tried to walk up to the barn by the driveway—out of respect. I thought Hugh was present and knew what my father and Stoelting did. Whenever I had visited a cemetery, I was told not to stand or walk over a grave. I hoped Hugh's ashes would be wafted up by the wind and out to the ocean. I imagined it could take years for that to happen. Maybe a hundred, I thought. I am still appalled by what my father did.

Just before Christmas, the saddle arrived. It was shipped in a heavy circular cardboard drum along with a bridle. A note from Mr. Stone stated the saddle was birch tanned and over time would turn a cherry-red color. It was perfect. The carved one-ear bridle had silver rosettas for holding a bit. Together they were quite grand. I carried a sawhorse from the barn for the saddle, and displayed it in our large front living room. Stoelting was furious when he saw it. He marched in a circle several times and stamped his feet as though he were acting. He mumbled in German under his breath and darted hateful looks at me. He clenched his fists and thrust them out as if to hit me. His stares were so toxic and evil, it seemed to me he stank from his icy blue eyes.

I put my hand on my saddle and said nothing; a shiver of fear spread across my shoulders. My heart pounded and then I became calm. He could do nothing. He turned angrily and stamped up the stairs to his room.

When my father came home, I explained to him why I wanted this type of saddle without silver. He admired it and ran a hand over the smooth leather. He said he understood! It was his Christmas present to me, and it was my best Christmas.

My mother invited Janet, my father's secretary, and her husband for Christmas dinner. She seemed to put away her anger toward Janet. This cheered my father. My brothers came too. Everyone enjoyed eating and drinking cocktails or wine. Dessert was a large gold cake with orange sugar icing and glasses of crème de menthe liquor. On that evening, Stoelting and Meuer celebrated Christmas somewhere in New York.

The saddle wasn't as important to others as it was to me. Meuer, my mother and her friend Marj, said they liked it, but weren't enthusiastic. I loved it, because I designed it and it had not one iota of a connection with Stoelting.

Chapter Twelve

MEETING JAN SHERWOOD AND A SHOT FIRED

My father, Stoelting and my older brother went to record companies and partied at the Plaza Hotel in New York with Miss Sherwood. The parties exposed her to people in the record industry. Stoelting coached her, how to act, when she met my mother and me. I believe he thought that if she acted as though she were inept on earth, our family would accept her as a new arrival from Venus.

One evening in January, 1957, when Meuer was away, Jan Sherwood arrived with Stoelting. My father, mother and I awaited her arrival. It was dark when we met them at our dimly lighted back door.

Stoelting barged in first to announce her, "This is the lovely Jan Sherwood."

The two made their way into the living room where Stoelting helped her remove a long plain, black, cashmere coat. He folded it preciously over the back of a chair. My mother glanced at her politely, but I couldn't help staring.

She was pale complected and appeared to be in her twenties. She wore her shiny black hair styled in a pixie cut. Thick, black mascara covered her long lashes. She sat daintily on the couch between my mother and me. She kept her body straight and turned her torso as though it were a swivel. She moved her head slowly from side to side as she looked about the room, staring curiously, as if she had never been in a house.

Stoelting spoke up, " Jan is getting acclimated to earth."

This caused her to blink and smile at him.

Our guest appeared unruffled and stiff. When she spoke she spoke in short sentences.

When asked questions she answered, "Yes, I think so." or just "Yes," or "No."

Stoelting told us she was learning to speak because on Venus they had no need– they communicated telepathically.

She wore cream–colored boots, tight, black pants with a matching tight blouse. A huge bracelet set with a large green stone covered much of her right wrist. Stoelting wore identical cream–colored boots. I surmised Clyde Stone the saddle maker in Salmon, Idaho had made them. This strange woman fascinated me. I searched for her specialness. I couldn't discern if she did or didn't come from Venus. She didn't have a German accent like Stoelting's. She had no accent at all. I wondered if Venusians might be really good at making themselves appear human. I didn't know. I didn't believe, nor did I disbelieve that she was an alien. She moved her head stiffly doll-like and stared wide-eyed at me. She repeated this movement with each sip of her coffee. I never saw anyone act in this manner.

Stoelting sat across from us smiling and jiggling his leg as he puffed on his leather–covered pipe. My father sat nearby in a maroon chair. He smiled and looked cheerfully at me and Miss Sherwood. My mother asked her how she liked living in Forest Hills. Miss Sherwood turned and looked at Stoelting questioningly, as if to ask what to say.

She bent her head to her chest and responded in a queer, high pitched voice, "I like it."

My father sensed tension and spoke of her recording ventures as a singer. I recall thinking, if she is learning to speak, how can she sing to make a record?

The five of us ate cake and drank coffee. Her short visit was bizarre. My father, Stoelting and the Venus woman left abruptly for a weekend in New York.

Afterwards, I asked my mother if she thought Jan Sherwood was beautiful. "I guess," she said.

"Is she from outer space?" I wanted to know.

"I don't know," she said.

I told her, "Dad thinks she is. He said so."

Perhaps at the time my mother wasn't sure either and maybe she didn't know. She and I were isolated from the so-called New York project. We didn't yet know the truth about what Stoelting, my father and Miss Sherwood were doing in New York. It was "hush hush."

Week after week, after the Venusian's visit, Stoelting and my father pressured my mother to go to New York to help Miss Sherwood adapt to living on earth. My mother thought the reasons weren't genuine. Stoelting said Jan needed help with recording debuts. My mother refused to go. She told me that she was afraid something bad might happen. I asked her what, but she gave no reason.

"I'd rather not say," she responded several times.

When Stoelting returned from his New York visits, my mother still folded his laundry as he had demonstrated, "Like so."

She continued knitting articles for his family and still sent money to them. She or I delivered Stoelting his breakfast in bed. She sat on the side of his bed transfixed, listening to his every word. Perhaps she was trying to find out more about the New York enterprise.

My mother became very depressed because of my father's affair and being excluded. My father continued to sleep in the same room as Stoelting even when he was away. My parents were becoming more estranged. My mother began taking Nebutal sleeping pills and pink Phenobarbital pills for daytime stress.

To avoid Stoelting, I ate breakfast in the kitchen by myself, or with Meuer. I couldn't mention Miss Sherwood's visit to Meuer because it was a secret, but I wondered just what she was.

Stockholder meetings were held regularly. My mother cleaned house on meeting days. Once a week, she hired a woman from the local Clinton Reformatory for Women. Women who were about to be released were hired out for cleaning or for light farm work. One of these women came to clean our house before a stockholder's meeting.

During the meetings, my mother and I served coffee and pastries on silver trays. My father, Stoelting, or Meuer motioned to us when more was needed. Serving people was a pleasant highlight.

After Christmas and the beginning of 1957 my mother rushed more than ever. When on the farm, she was always busy wanting the farm to be run efficiently. Before being married, she had been an efficiency expert for a stock brokerage firm in New York. She wanted tasks to be finished quickly and efficiently. Lunch was served at twelve noon, dinner at six o'clock. She had figured ways to do more work in less time. She ironed a shirt in three minutes. She busied herself cooking, cleaning and knitting and could turn a sock heel in an evening.

Besides her increased activity, she reverted to wearing black, as she had when her mother died. She told people, once again, that it was for the loss of her dead mother. Really it was because she had lost my father to Janet. It was a sign of her sadness.

She gave up drinking wine and smoking cigarettes as part of a pact she made with God. She wanted my father to give up Janet, and believed God would listen to her prayer, if she sacrificed. She increased her prayers. She went to church every Sunday and made novenas to the Virgin Mary. She prayed to St. Jude Thaddeus. She used her key to the local church and went there in evenings to pray. She lighted weekly candles, which flickered faithfully in our bathtub day and night. My father was bemused by her increased religiosity. Her petitions weren't working. She asked me to pray. I, too, went to church and prayed for my father to give up Janet. God seemed to be elsewhere.

Marj Kent visited often. Both she and my mother were widows in some respect. They both lamented the loss of their spouses. Marj was active in the local Protestant church. My mother wanted her prayers, too. Marj said she would pray.

Marj had been wise and didn't trust Stoelting. She never bought stock, but Willie Augstein, our neighbor did. He was the man who converted our garage into a barn.

Augstein, a bachelor, wanted to date Marj and asked her out for dinner. Stoelting had told him that she inherited a bundle of money. She owned the Barn Theater in Frenchtown, drove a new gray Buick, but was cagey about her money. She declined Augstein's invitation, and told my mother and me she didn't want to be involved with him because he was a laborer at The Taylor Wharton Iron and Steel and was unlike her deceased husband who was educated and a news reporter.

Marj often came to dinner when Stoelting was gone. She enjoyed Meuer's talks about his gold mining adventures in California. When Stoelting and Meuer sat at dinner, Meuer spoke little. Stoelting often gave him meaningful looks, signaling him not to talk. Stoelting wanted him to limit his conversation to mining. In retrospect it would have been disastrous for Stoelting, if Meuer or one of us had mentioned Jan Sherwood.

My father and Stoelting again tried to lure my mother to Forest Hills to help Jan Sherwood get ready for an imminent record company debut. Mother knew it was a ruse, and it was.

At dinner and after several glasses of wine, my father

criticized my mother. He faulted her clothes and cooking and laughed at her "blue blood" heritage– her family had documentable crests dating from the 1600s. She would then cry and he would say he was sorry. Then he told her he loved her and that he wished she understood the importance of Janet and of the outer space project.

Once she asked, "What does she have that I don't have?"

"Nothing, she just works it different," he said.

This was devastating. Her immediate reaction was to take two Nembutals and go to bed while clutching her crystal rosary. I kissed her that night, and then went tearfully to bed myself. Nights, I too, prayed and tried to visualize the Virgin Mary, because maybe she had the most power.

Stoelting had asked us to pray to his mother who was on Venus. He said he was Christ's brother.

My father would pour a glass of wine and raise it up to drink and say "to mother." My mother never did this, nor did I ever pray to his mother. I thought that was weird because Stoelting's mother couldn't possibly be holy!

Whenever Stoelting was present, when my parents fought, he excused himself and left for his bedroom. Tension floated about the house like a black acid cloud. When they fought, I felt as if I had swallowed lead. I tried my best to act calm, but my nerves were on edge. I was weary of the arguments and afraid of Stoelting. I loved my parents and wanted my life and theirs to change for the better. Later, each parent would tell me their side of the story and what their grief was and how they were right. Although I was fifteen, I tried to figure out how I could help.

When a reformatory woman was scheduled to clean, Meuer would take his gun which he kept in a brown paper bag in the small desk in the front room, unload it and place it back in the paper bag and put it back into the desk. He'd carry his gun when he left to pick up equipment or visit abandoned mines in New Jersey and Pennsylvania.

It was the end of March or the beginning of April, 1957 when I watched Meuer unload his gun and replace it in the bag inside the desk. The woman from the reformatory was coming to help my mother polish silver for a meeting on April 2nd. Meuer and Stoelting planned to present new developments.

That night, Marj Kent wanted Meuer to help her with her income tax after the meeting. She invited him to stay the night in her spare bedroom. He agreed, since he had just finished his own taxes and tax preparation was fresh in his mind.

After having dinner with us, Marj asked if I wanted to go with her to a church bazaar that evening. My mother gave me permission and I was happy to go. I wanted to know what a bazaar was. The church had long tables displaying embroidered handkerchiefs, piggy banks made from detergent bottles, crocheted hats and knitted mittens. Lining the sides of the tables were pot holders made from scraps of calico material and dolls fashioned from clothespins. The church women served punch and warm cider in paper cups. The bazaar gave me ideas about making things at home.

It was about nine o'clock when we came back from the church. The stockholder meeting was over. Meuer left with Marj to help her prepare her income tax. My mother was in the kitchen cleaning up when I went to bed. I was still sleeping in the front bedroom.

After sleeping for a couple of hours I got up to go to the bathroom. The landing from the living room stairs was in front of my bedroom door. Because of the airy winding of the steps, if one stood at the top of the stairs, they could easily hear conversation from below coming from the dining room or living room.

As I turned toward the bathroom I stopped as I heard voices coming from below. A chill stunned me as I heard Stoelting, "We have to do something about Jean. She refuses to come with us to New York. We have given her chance after chance. We have to get rid of her for the sake of the project. Do you think you can do it?"

"Yes," my father replied.

"See this? It's as thin as the air. You rub it on her head like so," Stoelting said. "Are you sure you can do it?"

"Yes."

I went back to my room and shut the door. I sat on the bed, cold and trembling. My bible sat under the lamp on my bedside table. I read something from Isaiah and prayed. I heard Stoelting and my father go up the back steps and into my brother's room to sleep.

I searched my brain frantically. What should or could I do? Stoelting and my father were planning to kill my mother. I have to do something. I must save her somehow. I knew Meuer's gun in the small desk in my same room was unloaded. I suddenly realized I could take the gun to scare Stoelting. This would let my father and him know I knew of their plot.

I opened the desk and lifted the paper bag and took out the gun. It was cold and heavy. I held it by my side and crept quietly down the hall, to the room where Stoelting and my father were sleeping. I knocked on the door. Someone said, "Come in." I was cold with fear. I hardly had strength to lift the latch on the door. Stoelting was in the bed nearest the door. He or I must have turned on the light.

I stood at the foot of his bed and said, "Thomas Stoelting, I know you are planning to kill my mother, and I am going to kill you." I held the gun up and pointed it at him. He sat up in bed and said, "Tony, we weren't talking about Jean were we?"

I said, "Yes, you were, and I know about putting some type of poison on my mother's head."

I held the gun firmly and waited for him to say something,

but the gun went off with a terrible, horrible, shattering bang. The noise shocked through my body. My father shouted, "My God! Sandy has shot Tom." I ran to my mother's room holding onto the gun and crying incoherently. I dropped the gun on the blanket chest in her room. "Hold me, just hold me, Dr. Tom wants to kill you." I repeated.

Clothed in her thin silky nightgown, she jumped up and grabbed her robe. I told her Dr. Tom and my father were planning to kill her because she wouldn't go to New York. I ran to her and hugged her trying to explain. I was crying hysterically. My mother called Dr. Boyer to come quickly. She grabbed my arm and the two of us rushed next door to get Harry Snyder, the town police officer. Someone called the rescue squad. Stoelting repeated it was an accident, and that I didn't mean to shoot him. After the rescue squad took Stoelting to the hospital, officer Snyder interviewed me. He wrote down everything. I told him everything I heard Stoelting and my father say. My father, who was standing nearby frowned at me and interjected, "Didn't you hear me say, 'But that's my wife and I love her'? He gave me a serious look. So, I told Officer Snyder that I heard him say, "But she's my wife and I love her."

An ambulance came shortly to take Stoelting to the hospital. Dr. Boyer came when the ambulance was leaving. He gave me an injection to calm me. I slept until the morning. When I awoke, I found myself lying on the couch in the living room.

Marj Kent came to the house with Meuer. She was mortified to find that Officer Snyder's report stated that Meuer was not in the house at the time of the shooting. She worried that she might be brought into the case as a witness and there would be gossip about a man staying overnight at her house. My father asked officer Snyder to add in his report that Meuer was sleeping in my room at the time of the shooting. I am not sure if officer Snyder did in fact change his initial report.

Stoelting was shot in the liver. Luckily he did not die. His liver was patched with a protein gel, and the bleeding stopped.

The day of the shooting, my mother and I told my father about the sexual abuse. I told him about the way Stoelting forced me to have sex the night of my grandmother's funeral, when he drove me home. I related how he forced me to have sex with him in the barn and how Dr. Hance treated me for gonorrhea, not a kidney infection. I told him I was sure I got the gonorrhea from Stoelting.

My father was furious that my mother hadn't told him, and that she had known about it for more than a year.

She told my father, "I didn't because when I asked Tom if he had sex with Sandy, he told me no."

My father asked me why I didn't tell him or Father Miller, the priest.

I told him, "I was afraid and no one would believe me." I told him Stoelting threatened to harm or to kill the two of them. My father shook his head and put his hands to his forehead and said, "We have to tell the police. Tom has to be charged with carnal abuse."

My father had gotten Stoelting to sign a statement that the shooting was an accident, which was fortunate. Stoelting had told detectives and the news reporters it was accidental. About a month later after several operations while Stoelting was still in the hospital, he was charged with carnal abuse.

Until that time, my father visited Stoelting every day and Stoelting claimed my father was his lawyer. I'm not sure why my father needed to visit him so often. Later, when he was discharged from the hospital, Stoelting was transferred to jail.

The papers were full of the shooting. My father would not talk to reporters. I don't think this was prudent, because Stoelting talked at length to them. He now told them I was a paramour of Meuer's and that Meuer and I had planned to kill him, since I shot him with Meuer's gun. My father told me not to read the papers but

I couldn't help reading some. Meuer moved out of our house immediately after the shooting. I don't know where he went to stay.

My father told my brothers to stay away, so none visited. Nor did my aunts or uncles. My brother Bob found out about the shooting from reading a newspaper on the way to work. My brother Tony visited Stoelting in the hospital but didn't visit our home. At the time he believed Stoelting and Jan were from outer space, believed I was evil, and that I tried to destroy something good.

My father too, believed Stoelting was from outer space and told me, "You've ruined everything." He believed he was working on a secret project with Stoelting. Even after I told him what Stoelting had done, I don't think he believed Stoelting infected me. I don't know whether my mother had told him earlier why I was being treated or if she stuck to the kidney infection story. She was the one who had Dr. Hance write a letter to the school stating that I was being treated for the kidney problem. She had believed the gonorrhea was encapsulated and had remained in my body from when I was eight years old.

My life was chaotic after the shooting. My parents didn't say much to me at all. Maybe they were figuring out how to proceed after all that happened. But I was so sad, lonely and unhappy. So many lies. I'm sure my father didn't corroborate the fact to my mother that Stoelting wanted to harm her, and that he had agreed to help him. Who would?

Because of the shooting, I was charged as a juvenile delinquent. Judge Harry W. Lindermann of Essex County presided over my private hearing. He said the shooting was "the culmination of what appears to be a very unusual and pathological interaction of five people in the Hauck household."

The result of the hearing was that my parents had custody of me, but the judge ruled the court had temporary jurisdiction over me. Jurisdiction changed back to my parents at the end of my junior high school year. I didn't understand this until now because this ruling was between the judge and my parents. They never told me about it. I discovered this recently from a court transcript.

After the shooting in the spring of 1957, I developed a femoral hernia, that pained me intermittently. I rode my horse and tried to ignore it for several months. It finally had to be operated and corrected. Dr. Hance did the surgery for the hernia before the trial. He never spoke to me about the gonorrhea infection.

Stoelting was in jail, but couldn't get a lawyer to defend him. No lawyer in New Jersey would defend him, because my father was well known and had been a prosecutor. Jules St. Germain of New York offered to take his case and got approved to practice in New Jersey.

Before the carnal abuse trial, the court ordered that I be examined. There were three examinations. The first was a vaginal examination by a doctor appointed by the state. My mother became frantic and was afraid the examination would reveal gonorrhea.

"I've got to do something," she said.

She phoned Dr. Hance. He suggested that I douche the day of the examination with an iodine solution. I most likely didn't have gonorrhea because I had no sex with Stoelting for months and had tested negative. Nevertheless, I douched with the solution. My mother took me to a large clinic for the test. I was gowned and ushered barefooted down a cold marble floor. The examination was probably to determine if I was as virgin as well as a test for disease.

Next, I met with two young men, who I suppose were psychologists. One asked me questions about the abuse while the other sat observing me.

One said, "Well, if this sex stuff went on for so long, you must have enjoyed it!"

I sobbed and told them that it was terrible. The man who said that pushed a box of Kleenex at my face.

Someone drove me to a psychological testing building in a huge brownstone in Long Island. It must have been my mother, but I can't remember just who it was. The building had large rooms, high ceilings and a marble fireplace. I was given an ink blot test with pictures of black blobs on cards. I was then requested to draw several items: a tree, a man and something else. At lunch time, I was told to get something to eat at a nearby White Castle restaurant. Coming from a small town, I had never bought lunch from people I didn't know. I managed to order something and walked back up a hill to the brownstone.

Neither of my parents asked me what these tests were, my experience or what happened. It was just something I had to do. In retrospect, I marvel at their detachment.

It was late September or early October when the carnal abuse trial finally started. The courtroom was filled. People shuffled their feet and talked noisily. Jules St Germain, Stoelting's lawyer, was big and brusk. He had a walrus-like mustache, strutted, swayed his body and flailed his arms when he approached the judge.

Herbert Heisel, the prosecutor and my lawyer, was slight and soft spoken. He told me not to be afraid just tell the truth about what Stoelting had done.

The courthouse suddenly became quiet. Stoelting was arriving.

Stoelting rode in a wheelchair, wrapped in a blanket. He sat at a table directly across from the witness stand. I still was terrified of him.

During the trial, on October 3, my mother testified under cross examination that I had told her in February 1956, about Stoelting's attacks, but stated she did not have me examined by a physician or ask where or when the attacks occurred. She also testified that she had knitted a pair of wool socks for Stoelting and sent him flowers when he was hospitalized after I shot him. She also said she had invited him to return to the our home when he was released from the hospital.

I testified for a day and a half, telling what Stoelting had done. I was confused about the exact date when Stoelting raped me in the barn. A local veterinarian testified my horse couldn't have been stabled in our barn because he had treated the horse at that time when it was boarded in town. This certainly made me look like a liar.

The worst testimony was when I had to relate how Stoelting wanted me to put my mouth to his penis. I cried. Stoelting sat across from me making grimaces as I testified about this and banged his fist on the table in front of him.

Rolf Meuer testified that Stoelting had told him about having sexual relations with me. He might have because the two of them were partners. But why didn't Meuer tell my parents? Did he plan to have sex with me too?

Stoelting's lawyer got two neighbors to testify they had seen me and Meurer having sex from the windows of Ora Thompson's house. Her house was next to ours. They said they saw the two of us from Ora's attic window. Our lawyers didn't contest this or go to her house to prove that this was impossible.

Stoelting, weak and thin, took the stand. He sat on a chair padded with blankets and told of his "fatherly" affection for me, and said he learned from Meuer of Meuer's love for me. These lies were numbing and frightening. But not as terrible as the awful deed my brother Tony did. I had been testifying for the second day about Stoelting's threats of harming my parents. St. Germain asked me if I had ever had intercourse with anyone prior to the alleged abuse by Stoelting. "No." I responded.

I clearly remember that I was wearing my favorite, gray,

woolen dress, and green flats when St. Germain then asked to approach the bench with the prosecutor, Herbert Heisel. Jules St. Germain had a piece of paper in his hand. It was a letter to Stoelting written by my brother, Tony. It was a lie letter. The letter stated that he had intercourse with me when my parents were on vacation in Pine Hurst, North Carolina. The letter was not admitted as evidence, but I was devastated. This lie my brother wrote has stuck like a black dart in my heart my whole life, even though he told me years later how sorry he was.

The world was against me. My father had been visiting Stoelting daily in the hospital before the trial, even though he knew what Stoelting had done. Perhaps he had been discussing outer space stuff. My mother had sent flowers and knitted socks for him. Not even Dr. Hance could testify that he had treated me for gonorrhea because he had written a letter to the school stating I was being treated for a kidney infection. I had also lost a whole year of high school.

Stoelting told reporters that he was Jewish and that my father was German and anti-Semitic. (In 1989, I found the Haucks were Jewish.) After that was publicized, when I walked up to testify, people sitting in the front row of the courtroom hissed at me. I can't find the words for the sadness I felt. It was beyond sad.

Robert Hicks, a lawyer from Washington, D.C., who had been an investigator on the Lindbergh-Hauptmann case, came north to help us. He had connections with a forensic lab in D.C. and wanted to find anything of interest about Stoelting. My mother and he found an overnight case of Stoelting's in the bedroom, in our house. They discovered a cylinder of reddish pressed powder. Hicks thought it might be a powder to rub on a man's face before shaving with an electric razor. He wanted to take this to the forensic lab. My mother wanted a sample and took it to the kitchen and cut a slice from one end to keep. Hicks told me to look around the barn, and also look for disturbed earth that might indicate something had been buried. I searched in the barn and found two small bottles buried near the hay bales. Each had liquid in it. Hicks took the powdered cylinder, the locket that Stoelting had filled with ground rock, the two bottles and the bracelet Stoelting had soldered on my wrist. This is the bracelet that had holes drilled in the side and plugged with a copper-colored metal.

Hicks had the liquid from the bottles tested. It was harmless. The holes in my bracelet were filled with a type of granular material like sand. The ground rock inside the locket was a type of granite. X-rays showed the cylinder from the bedroom had a hollow chamber. The chamber was filled with cyanide crystals. My mother had cut the cylinder very close to the end. Luckily she cut a small piece. Hicks was excited about the find and wanted the items and report submitted as evidence. They were not.

Richard Harpster, a reporter for the now defunct Newark Evening News, told the Hunterdon Review Newspaper in May of 1989, that the case became an obsession for him and fellow reporter Bruce Hotchkiss. Hotchkiss became an editor of the Review in the late '60s. The two had written dozens of letters and telegrams trying to check into Stoelting, whom they suspected of being a brilliant confidence man. They checked aliases, immigration authorities, the Securities Exchange Commission, and the Bureau of Mines. Their research led them to California, Idaho, Utah, Nevada, Arizona and Washington. They learned the geologist had been arrested several times in the west by the immigration department, but the department would not reveal the details.

They discovered a story from Bakersfield, California about Stoelting as a "lieutenant" in a group known as the American Military Reserve, which was set up in 1941 in the Mojave desert as an army. It was broken up by the FBI.

Reporters were intrigued by Stoelting. "He could charm anyone," Harpster said. "A president of a gold mine, the charismatic uranium mine stock salesman could convince people of anything," Harpster said.

Finally the trial was over. The jury couldn't imagine how Stoelting was before he was shot. They couldn't believe he could abuse me several times a week. They believed he was Jewish. Many times, when we lived on the farm, he had eaten <u>raw</u> bacon sandwiches. I had heard him once tell Willie Augstein, "A good Jew is a dead Jew." I doubt he was Jewish!

On October 12, the jury was sent to deliberate on the charge against Stoelting and returned almost immediately with the verdict of innocent. "Women wept openly and rushed to congratulate Stoelting and his attorneys. People on the streets rushed into the courthouse to shake hands with the weeping Stoelting," according to the Newark News.

I was bereft of understanding. The jury did not believe me. My parents said, "Don't think about it so much." I did think about the trial. When I shut my eyes, I could see Stoelting squinting hatefully at me as he had done in court.

This was just the beginning of my grief to come.

Chapter Thirteen

FALL 1957 –
THE CONVENT SCHOOL

Although the carnal abuse trial was past, I soon learned that the harrowing effects of the trial did not remain locked away in the courthouse. I needed to go back to school. I had already lost my sophomore year because of being absent. I thought I would just go back to my high school in Annandale, New Jersey. But, Judge Lindermann did not want me to return to the local high school.

Instead, I enrolled at a Roman Catholic academy in Peapack-Gladstone, New Jersey. One section of the school was for boys and another for girls. My mother bought uniforms which were green jumpers and white nylon blouses. A shiny yellow bus with brown plastic-covered seats transported me to my new school. Crisp leaves and the cool air of late fall invigorated me that first day. A good change awaited me, and I was ready for a change.

I also corrected my name on my birth certificate to Alexandra, as it was supposed to have been when I was born. When my mother was in labor, she was doped up with something called "twilight sleep." As a result my birth certificate was issued as Sandra instead of Alexandra. My parents and others persisted calling me Sandra or Sandy since it was my legal name. My mother liked the name Sandy because my hair color was a light sandy-yellow. My name was something I could change and was not identified with my horrid past.

I was ready for a new school with a new name. On the first day of school, I began conversational Italian. A chubby, short nun taught the class. Every minute in this school was exciting. The students seemed happy. On the bus ride home a student who sat in front of me was particularly friendly. She wore her hair in a long singular braid. The very tip had a smart bright ribbon. Her name was Mitae. I thought she and I might become friends.

When my father came home from work that Friday, he said, "You can't go back to the school. The parents don't want you. It's because of all the publicity. Don't worry, we'll find something."

I was shattered. I rushed upstairs to cry. I cried until I was cried out, until I had no more tears.

During the next week my parents and I visited a private boarding school in Maryland. Large trees and well trimmed lawns surrounded beautiful brick buildings. After I walked around the grounds, the dean interviewed me. He said, "You wouldn't fit in here. The students here come from very rich families." He was right. I wouldn't.

That very same week, Father Zaliski, the local priest, came to dinner. He said his sister was a nun and knew of a convent school in Syosset, Long Island. He thought it would be a good school for me.

Again we traveled in hopes of finding a school. The convent was run by Mercy nuns, a teaching order. The front of the brown stone building was dreary with a heavy, huge wooden door. We were greeted by a nun. We walked up several marble steps and were directed to wait in a large room with antique chairs and oriental rugs. The building's brown shellacked woodwork was depressing. We sat in silence awaiting the Mother Superior, Sister Mary Eileen. We heard her clothes rustling and her rosary beads clicking as she approached. A tall, willowy-thin, pale nun in a black habit halted in the doorway. She swung her arms out and clapped enthusiastically. "You must be Alexandra." She said I would love it at Our Lady of Mercy Academy. She asked me if I thought I would like it there. I had no idea about that. The nun spoke about the convent as if it were a marvelous place. I might even go horseback riding. I would need jodhpurs and boots. Green uniforms would be ordered. The sister handed my mother a clothing list and directions for ordering name tags.

Sister Eileen thought I would be a good student and would enjoy the friendship of the other sophomore boarders. She affirmed that she would be the only one who knew about my past, and promised not to tell the other nuns about it. She kept her promise, but I encountered other obstacles to my happiness.

A court order barred me from going home until the end of the school year. That included the Christmas, New Year and Easter holidays. My father said he could do nothing. I wanted a better life. I felt abandoned and believed I was being punished.

In retrospect, I believe Judge Lindermann was protecting me, and most likely wanted me far from the small town of Clinton, New Jersey.

The week after the interview, I arrived at school. My parents were allowed to accompany me to the upstairs sleeping quarters which consisted of large room divided into cubicles. Each boarder occupied an eight-foot square. Mine was in a corner and had two large windows. It was furnished with a springy bed, a straight back chair and a dresser. A large, oak-framed tipping mirror was attached to the back of the dresser. There were no other mirrors throughout the convent except those in our cubicles. Admiring yourself in a mirror was prideful, and pride was a sin. A thick white curtain was used to close the open side of the cubical for privacy.

Sister Mary Felicitas, a tittering, aged, pale nun, was in charge of the dorm. She watched me unpack while my parents looked on. She made sure I had nothing not allowed. Flashlights and food were not allowed. I brought two green woolen blankets, a pillow, sheets and a bedspread as well as my clothes.

Stoelting had been using one of the blankets the night of the shooting. My mother had darned the bullet hole with green wool. We certainly had other blankets that I could have used; I don't think my mother thought about its possible affect on me, but I was well aware of its presence—and its recent history.

That evening, my parents and I dined at a local restaurant. I couldn't eat. They left me at the convent door sobbing. A nun ushered me into a "rec" room, short for recreation, where I was introduced to the other boarders. One boarder played "Chopsticks" and "Heart and Soul" on an old upright piano. A tattered couch and several chairs lined the wall. Drab green curtains bordered cold, wintery window panes. A Victrola record player for 78 rpm records sat on a large table with stacks of records and boxes of puzzles. A couple of boarders were writing letters at the table end.

Eventually we lined up silently along the hall outside the room. We covered our heads with green caps or prayer veils and shuffled over the polished marble floor to the chapel. We knelt in dark wooden pews. Flickering candles shadow danced us against the cream-colored ceiling and walls. We repeated prayers and lastly the Memorare prayer after the nun. A short silence gave us the opportunity to pray for our own petitions. We were instructed to maintain silence until after breakfast the next day. However, we whispered at night after we were sure Sister Felicitas had gone to bed.

Sister Felicitas woke us at 6:30. She rang a large bell as she walked past our cubicles. We washed, dressed and aired our beds, then followed the sister silently to breakfast.

My favorite breakfast was cocoa and sugar bread. I discovered a buttered, sugared roll was especially delicious when accompanied by several cups of cocoa. Of course, I gained weight rapidly. After breakfast, we made our beds and rushed to study hall before classes. Students in the convent shared classes with local residents who were called "day students." The nuns cautioned us not to give letters to these students for mailing. We would be expelled if we violated the rule. All boarders' mail, incoming and outgoing, was read by a nun. I once wrote to my mother that I was sad and wanted to go home. Sister Inocencia read the letter and told me that I couldn't write that. It would upset my mother. So, I rewrote a letter stating everything was going well, and I was enjoying my studies.

After school we had free time. We went to our cubicles or to the "rec" room. We could buy candy from one of the nuns. After dinner we went to study hall for the second time, then we retired to the "rec" room only to repeat the ritual of praying in the chapel and heading silently to bed. As a rule we weren't allowed outside. Occasionally, several of us begged a nun for a walk around a pond that was on the convent grounds. They were busy too, saying their prayers or sewing their habits by hand. I did go horseback riding twice with other students. I wanted to go again, but I was told that riding in cold weather wasn't healthy.

Studying and reading *Main-Travelled Roads*, a book by Hamlin Garland, kept me sane. One part of the book describes how he returned to his farm and rolled in the sod because he was so happy to be home. I wanted to do the same thing.

Tuesday evenings, I was allowed to telephone home. A nun always listened nearby. Week after week, I begged my father to allow me to come home. I couldn't understand why he was unable to get me out.

Sister Mary Carmel, the English teacher, and Sister Pierre, who taught French both thought I would make an excellent nun. I didn't want to be a nun. They told me they were just like me in that, they too, liked horses. Most of the nuns were patient except for the math teacher. She terrorized me when I went to the blackboard. I just couldn't do math at the front of the class. I told her I did know it, but she didn't believe me until I got 98 percent in the state math test.

She said, "Why, you did know it all along."

Art was my favorite class. I had it every day. Every day, we knelt and prayed for President Eisenhower. I prayed to get out of there and go home to be with my horse and things that were familiar.

That year was grueling. My mother came to visit most weekends. I waited in the "rec" room for her to arrive. She drove out on Saturday mornings to pick me up. I was so happy to see her at the huge convent door. She dressed beautifully. She often wore her black Persian lamb coat and smelled of Shalimar perfume. I had to return by seven. Sunday mornings, she again collected me. We sometimes walked about neighboring towns. After my mother picked me up on Sundays, I waited in the car and listened to the radio while she attended a Catholic mass in a nearby church.

The room where she slept at the Anchorage Motel in Cold Spring Harbor, had a tiny refrigerator and stove. My mother always prepared the same food for herself and me. Ham sandwiches for lunch. Dinner consisted of cubed steaks and salad with wishbone dressing, followed by cake.

During her visits, she cried about my father's affair and how lonely she was. I was helpless to comfort her and wanted only to go home. My horse was at home. I hadn't seen my horse for the longest time and wanted a picture of him. She promised me she would send me one. She and Willie Augstein had been feeding and caring for him.

We didn't talk about Stoelting or the trial. She focused on my father's affair and added that she missed having me at home.

The boarders were curious because I did not go home for weekends. Even students from Puerto Rico went to relatives in Queens. I told them that my parents were having marital problems. Irene M. a boarder, thought I was mysterious and some kind of undercover agent.

My mother and I spent Thanksgiving dinner with the Faulkensteins who owned the motel. I stayed overnights in the motel with my mother during the school holiday. We visited horse stables at a nearby estate. The barn had tile floors and polished brass bars on the stall doors. The horses looked comfy. I would have very much liked to stay there, with those horses, instead of at the convent.

I didn't see my father during the holiday, but he came one Saturday in December. I had gained 20 pounds, going from 125 to 145 pounds. He said he was disappointed at how fat I had become. He stayed for lunch with my mother and me in the motel room. The gray and overcast sky added sadness to his visit. He left abruptly to see a client. He walked back across the gravel to his car and waved good bye to my mother, who stood at the motel door. A blustery, cold wind flapped his gray, wool overcoat. I asked him to stay longer. I stroked his scarf and hugged him. He said, "Keep your chin up," then gave me a kiss before driving off.

Christmas was coming. My father told me that even though I was not allowed home, I could go to my aunt's in Plainfield, New Jersey for the holiday. I could hardly wait to pack. I would be gone for two weeks. Hooray. When I arrived to stay at my Aunt Marion's, it was not what I had expected. She greeted me with a quick hug, and there was no joy in her smile. She seemed nervous. My mother didn't stay. She was returning home, but promised to come back on Christmas Day to bring presents. I thought my father might visit, too.

My two aunts, Marion and Ruth, were superficially happy to see me. Uncle Jack, my mother's brother, drove me around the town of Plainfield to see the Christmas lights and decorations. His wife, Aunt Helen, didn't come. I sat in the front seat while my uncle pointed out areas he liked. I was bored and lonely. I didn't care about Christmas. I was only thirty miles from my home and couldn't go. It seemed my relatives interacted with me because it was the "good Christian" thing to do. I had twenty dollars. Uncle Jack took me shopping to get presents for my parents and Aunt Marion.

On Christmas Day, I attended an Episcopal service with my aunts, uncles and cousins. No one spoke about what had happened or inquired about school. My relatives did their best to treat me as if nothing had changed. Conversations were light and focused on how my aunt intended to fix up her house, how much her new Olympia typewriter cost and how it typed in script. My relatives' false cheerfulness and trivial laughter added to my loneliness. My mother came Christmas afternoon. She had spent the morning celebrating with my father, who then went to celebrate Christmas with Janet, his secretary, and her adoptive relatives. My father was too busy to come.

I wanted and got a pair of black-and-white saddle shoes with pink soles for school. I also received a camel hair coat and other presents including a leather manicure kit. My mother returned to our house in Clinton, while I stayed with my aunt Marion.

Aunt Marion allowed me to use her new typewriter. I walked about the neighborhood near my aunt's house and helped her prepare food. She owned many first edition books and illuminated manuscripts dating from the 1500's. These were unlocked for me to carefully examine. All her belongings were precious and special. A beautiful, woven shahrukh oriental carpet covered her living room floor. My aunt showed me the closely tied knots on the underside. A large number of knots per square inch made the rug especially rare. Antique porcelains, music boxes and a handmade canopy bed were museum quality.

Aunt Ruth came in the evenings and read from *Pooh Bear* and *Thomasina The Cat Who Thought She was God*. My mother came to stay for several days and my father visited one evening for dinner.

I was sorry to return to the convent. I hadn't gone home and I hated goodbyes. It seemed my entire life was peppered with them ever since I could remember. My mother and others were always going somewhere and I wasn't going. I would be alone again with that dark crinkly feeling of dread. I hated the passing of time, and checked my watch as if to hold onto every last minute before being left at the convent door. Desperately, I tried not to cry and to keep my chin up as my father had instructed.

I pretended my holiday was a good one, but I choked back tears. The other boarders said they had a great time. Even Rosario P. had returned to Venezuela. Her father didn't like the fact that she had gained weight either.

Eventually, I became used to the school routine. However, I would still cry at night for home. I was lucky to have a window from which to see the moon and snow far below. I greedily captured the moon light, and often sat on my bed and looked up at the night sky. I would recall my life on the farm, how I had slept outside on hot summer nights and searched the sky for twinkling stars. Unable to capture this feeling of home and happiness for long, I nonetheless tried to bring it to mind before falling asleep.

I prayed to various saints. I imagined and hoped they were lined up just waiting for me to call upon them for help. I reviewed them in my mind. Perhaps I wasn't humble enough or didn't pray in a proper manner. Was that why my prayers weren't answered? The sisters told us many times that all of us were there to save our souls. Our souls were more important than our grades. The best thing to be was a nun, but you had to know the calling. I felt I wasn't good enough to be a nun. I felt I was tainted. In retrospect, I was really naive to think that way.

I had such little contact with home, my possessions at school became beloved. My travel clock with a plastic roll cover, my dresser scarf, the socks my mother had sewn with name tags, my hair brush, and any other item that reminded me of home. My meager posses-sions and I had been displaced to a foreign location. It was as if I had to embrace my belongings because my world had become isolated and separate. They were all I had.

Month after month, my mother tried to come and visit with me on weekends. May was the Virgin Mary's month. The students made a procession around a statue of Mary and knelt to pray to her. We wore white dresses and white shoes in her honor. Real flower wreaths were placed on our heads by the nuns. Mary's statue had a flower wreath placed on her head, too. The perfume from the blooming flower beds and in our hair made us students giddy. The school year ended on the last day of May. Yippee! School didn't seem so bad now. Tuesday night when I called home, I made sure my mother knew that I could go home Saturday for good.

It was spring in 1958. My life was going to be good. My mother and a family friend, Francis Decleene, came to pick me up. I had packed and neatly folded my blankets and sheets in a pile at the foot of the bed. I didn't care to have any ties with the other students or the school. I was still leery that others would find out about my past and judge me as evil. I knew that would make me feel worse than I did already. I wanted to cut ties entirely with the bad memories of the school because I never wanted to be there at all. I couldn't get away fast enough.

The ride home was like a dream. I gazed out the window to gobble up roadside scenes with my eyes. The three of us stopped at a Howard Johnson's restaurant for lunch.

Once home, I ran to see Woozer, my horse and give him hugs. I had gotten him before I ordered the saddle from Clyde Stone. Ted Smith from Asbury, New Jersey found Woozer, and I swapped Foxie, who was better for a lighter rider than I. Since I had been gone, Woozer's hooves grew quite long. He needed to be shod before I could ride him again. When my father returned to the house that evening, it was as if I hadn't been gone at all.

After he kissed me on the cheek, he asked, "How are you? And how was the trip?" I told him it was fine and that Woozer needed a ferrier. He said he would call one.

I roamed about the house that now felt so strange. There was no sign of Stoelting or Meuer. My brother's room where Stoelting had slept looked the same as it had before he had arrived. The clean room smelled of Pine-Sol and wax. There was no smell of tobacco or other hints of him. Every room seemed new. My closet had clothes that no longer fit. I tried on my jeans and could not zip them. I was too busty for my western shirts. I was fat. Monday, my mother took me shopping for clothes. She said, "What's past is past." This cautioned me to fit in and be ordinary. I was like a coyote cub returning to the pack after a long absence. My parents were accustomed to my absence and accepted me back into the family slowly. I started riding again and caring for my horse.

That summer in 1958, much to my dismay, there was another trial.

Chapter Fourteen

THE SECOND TRIAL

Stoelting filed a negligence lawsuit

against my parents and me, immediately after his acquittal of the carnal abuse. My parents and I were now defendants. The trial was about us. My father told my brothers to stay away during the first trial. They did. Recently while talking to my brothers, they didn't even know, or remember, that there was a second trial, until I told them. They said they were unaware. I don't know who my father was trying to protect by telling my brothers to stay away–me or them.

Jules St. Germain was again Stoelting's lawyer. Allen Mathias was ours.

There was a pretrial hearing in May, 1958. This was a hearing before Judge Gerald Foley without a jury. During the hearing, the lawyers discussed and agreed upon what could be admitted for the upcoming trial. Judge Foley then wrote an order for the lawyers which provided the boundaries of the lawsuit.

My father cautioned me, "Don't mention anything about outer space. That's not important to the trial and it would make us look mentally deranged."

It was still a secret.

We did not deny that Stoelting was shot. Stoelting alleged that my parents and I were negligent and that caused his injuries. We countersued, contending that Stoelting had contributory negligence. Since he contended I was dangerous, we argued that he, as a prudent person, should not have stayed at our house.

The purpose of Stoelting's lawsuit was to obtain payment for his injuries and compensation for his pain and suffering.

The trial, starting on June 24th, was eleven days of hot summer hell. Stoelting walked in wearing a baggy gray suit and tie, both much too large for him. He appeared thin and strained from the heat. It was not a surprise that Stoelting lied. He said he saw me practicing quick draws with Meuer's .45-caliber pistol, the gun with which he was shot. He claimed he told my mother, who did nothing about this. He described a photograph of me pointing Meuer's gun, and even subpoenaed Meuer to produce the photograph. Although there was no such photo, Judge Foley allowed Stoelting to describe one.

Because of this testimony, several newspapers described me as a "gun moll." When I heard this disturbing lie, apprehension and terrible dread made my heart sink. There was a photograph of me pointing my father's revolver. It was the one I used for target practice the time I went with Sheriff Lea, his daughter and Meuer. Both Stoelting and Meuer had wanted me to know how to shoot a gun because rattlesnakes and cougars lived in the Idaho mountains. Stoelting had suggested I visit Idaho. Both Stoelting and Meuer described long-horned sheep and roaming wild horses. After hearing their stories, I had been eager to go there someday.

When Stoelting was on the witness stand, he was asked if he said he wanted me to learn to shoot because of the dangers out west. He denied that. My parents, who knew this to be so, didn't testify about that.

The photograph of me pointing my father's gun was introduced as evidence. Stoelting got this photo by way of my father! A roll of film from my father's camera had pictures of Idaho but at the end of the roll, there were two pictures of me with a gun.

In May, before the trial, my father and his secretary Janet, visited Stoelting and gave him the pictures and the roll of negatives.

I was shocked when years later I read this from the trial transcript. I had always wondered how Stoelting got the pictures, because I didn't know they existed.

My father testified that he had never seen the pictures of me, and did not know who took them, or how they came from a roll of film on his camera. The fact that he went to see Stoelting in May before the shooting trial made me think my father believed Stoelting more than he did me. Why did he and Janet visit him? It seemed the world was still against me, and I could not do anything. A quagmire of one thing after the other made me appear to be an evil teen.

At the trial, I tried not to look at the jurors. Ten men and two women were in the jury box. I could feel them studying and judging me. Occasionally, I glanced at them and saw them nod their heads, usually in agreement with St. Germain's statements.

Everyday was hot and sticky. My bare legs beneath my cotton dresses stuck to the shellacked benches. The courtroom had fans but no air conditioning. Occasionally, a light breeze came through an open window. The jurors, although nearer the windows, shifted often and wiped their perspiring heads. My heart was always in my throat, but I had to maintain a calm appearance. I wanted to jump up and confront Stoelting as a liar, but I knew I shouldn't. Instead, I stuffed it all away, as I had always done. This made me dull-brained and sleepy. Inside, I was in a stupor.

After the court recessed and we returned home each evening, my father cautioned me not to read the newspapers or to think about the harrowing day. I didn't read the newspapers, but I did mull over the lies from Stoelting. My stomach was in knots because I was being judged again. Those evenings in my room, I tried to read. I needed to read a paragraph over many times to understand it.

My mother was stressed because she had been subpoenaed by St. Germain to testify. My father wasn't too upset. He still believed that Stoelting had a higher mission from outer space for him.

He told me that, "By shooting Stoelting, you've ruined everything."

My mother said, "I understand you were protecting me."

I knew that the outer space thing was fake. The convent did something for me. I now had a deep faith in God. I had an ally. I had survived my past and the first terrible trial. I prayed because I was so alone. I wanted to get through this trial and with the grace of God, I thought I might.

Meuer testified that Stoelting had given him his gun. The lawyers approached the judge's bench. Meuer wanted to testify that Stoelting asked him to always keep his gun loaded. He had told Meuer that he met little green men in the Mojave desert, who were from outer space, and he was afraid for his life. Stoelting's lawyer objected to that statement and the jury did not hear it.

Stoelting had his own gun on the dresser in his bedroom the time of the shooting. I had testified to that fact. My mother did not tell the detectives on the day of the shooting that she had removed Stoelting's gun and hidden it. She did this immediately after Stoelting was shot. She testified that she put it under her clothes in her dresser drawer. St. Germain tried to prove that was a lie. Stoelting testified that his gun was somewhere else, but did not say just where his gun was. A photograph of a holster on Stoelting's dresser was produced by a detective. Judge Foley did not allow Stoelting to say more about his gun despite our lawyer's objections. He said it did not pertain to the shooting itself.

St. Germain, Stoelting's lawyer, made countless objections to evidence our lawyer wanted to admit. Judge Foley sustained the objections in Stoelting's favor.

We found someone contacted the FBI concerning Stoelting's activities. Our lawyers subpoenaed FBI information on Stoelting. Two young male agents came to the courthouse carrying a briefcase. One took out a thick file. I presumed it was Stoelting's. They approached the judge's bench with the lawyers. After a few minutes the two men left. Our lawyer later told us the agents could only testify to the fact that they had a file on Stoelting. Oddly, when my senior high school class visited the FBI building in Washington, D.C., one of the same agents that was at the trial two years earlier spoke about the FBI to our class! I gave him a knowing, puzzled look. He returned a slight smile and a nod. I thought it strange that he should be there. Because of that occurrence, I believed the FBI was protecting me.

During the trial, a ballistics expert testified that the gun I shot was found to have a "light pull" on the trigger.

Doctor after doctor testified about Stoelting's injuries from the bullet. He was hospitalized for about three months. His injured liver was repaired with Gelfoam, a protein-like gel. Our lawyer, Allen Mathias brought out the fact that he had previous chest injuries from an army tank rollover and that not all his suffering was caused from the bullet. Information about the injuries from the tank rollover was admitted, but not the information that they occurred during the time Stoelting had formed an illegal ragtag army in the Mojave Desert. The army was formed in the 1940s and was broken up by the FBI.

Stoelting had spent a week in a California jail and some time in a sanitarium. He previously testified that he was never in jail, and only visited the sanitarium. The sanitarium records were too far back to prove he had a lung condition.

When in court, Stoelting, although very thin, managed to walk and use his arms well. Stoelting's doctors testified that he was totally disabled, and our expert witness stated he was not totally disabled because he could still sit at a desk and sell stock. All this was tedious and boring, but necessary for the trial to end.

I was not allowed to testify about the actual conversation I heard by the stairway between Stoelting and my father–the conversation about killing my mother. I was not called as a witness by our lawyer. If I had testified, my father would have had to testify about the conversation and he didn't want to testify why he was sleeping in the same room with Stoelting, either.

Because Stoelting's lawyer had subpoenaed me, I could only testify that I had heard 'a conversation' and then took the gun to scare Stoelting. For sure, this made me look like an idiot.

Stoelting claimed he was a mining engineer and got $75 a day when working for the Dixie-Cup company. He did work there for a few weeks in 1950, and was paid $75 a day.

It is my understanding that Dr. Hance's son got Stoelting the job. Stoelting had boasted that he knew a way to seal the cups by changing the molecular structure of paper. He didn't. Dr. Hance's son and Stoelting were both fired. Stoelting didn't testify that he was fired. He testified that he couldn't talk about the job because he didn't have the approval of the Dixie-Cup Company—it was proprietary research!

Our lawyer found evidence showing Stoelting used Meuer to lie about how much time the two really spent staking claims. Letters from Stoelting to Meuer were not admitted but were used later by our lawyer.

Stoelting kept 51% of stock sales. He claimed he got his income from mining and staking claims. Our lawyer tried to prove that Stoelting had conned people for years. Company after company went bankrupt because he only made money from stock sales and did not mine or prospect for ore. St. Germain objected. Judge Foley ruled that the sale of stock was still related to mining.

When Stoelting was in New Jersey, he wrote a letter to Meuer who was in California. He begged Meuer not to tell that while the two were in Idaho for three months they had only worked one day. Stoelting also wrote and told Meuer not to say anything negative on the phone, if Stoelting mentioned his birth date. That would mean that my father would be listening in on an extension phone. Stoelting wrote that if the mine wasn't going well, my father would drop it like a hot potato. The letter stated he would call Meuer back in an hour to find out what was really going on. Stoelting frequently asked my father to listen when he called Meuer. St. Germain responded to this letter, arguing that perhaps my father was an eavesdropper. Some of this letter was permitted, but not all of it.

Judge Foley prohibited a lot of evidence and testimony. He said he wanted to keep the trial limited to the shooting.

After all the testimony and exhibits, the jury found the three of us negligent. They awarded Stoelting a striking amount of $100,000. The jury had the option to determine that I was a juvenile delinquent, but thankfully, they did not.

Later evidence not admitted at the trial in our defense was presented for a settlement out of court. The bracelet that Stoelting had soldered on my wrist and the locket he forced me to wear as "charms" were used to demonstrate Stoelting's efforts to control me. The bracelet was the one that had holes plugged with metal and the locket that had pulverized rock glued inside. These were supposed to protect me from evil outer space aliens. A forensic report on the pressed powder cylinder was also used. A Washington, D.C. laboratory reported cyanide crystals were in a hollowed out portion. Other evidence was used as our defense to lower the initial jury award to Stoelting. On July 23, 1960, three years after Stoelting was shot, a settlement of $55,000 was reached, overturning the original one of $100,000. In addition, our insurance paid a large amount of money to the hospital where Stoelting was treated. By the time of the settlement, I had just graduated from high school.

Chapter Fifteen

PUBLIC HIGH SCHOOL AND NURSING

After the trial ended in July, my father bought a bungalow on the outskirts of Clinton, New Jersey. The property had a barn and corral for my horse, Woozer.

Before we moved in, my mother and I cleaned the entire house with a Lysol solution, because the house had been vacant for several months.

For the first time, I had a spacious bedroom. One westward window faced several impressive fir trees. I often watched the sun set between them, as it lowered into the far-off cornfield.

I was happy we moved away from 56 West Main Street, where our neighbor and her friend had lied at the trial and testified they saw me and Meuer having sex. Although the horridness of my life seemed past, I was a nervous wreck. I believed I was destined for an unhappy and tragic future.

After the trials and my stint in the convent, I was determined to make my life work. I rode my horse and painted with watercolors. I explored Eastern religions. I read *The Autobiography of a Yogi*, the Indian epic, *The Bhagavad-Gita*, *The Upanishads* and *The Tibetan Book of the Dead*. I also read Mormon religious books: *The Pearl of Great Price* and *The Book of Mormon*. I was eager to learn about beliefs that were different from what I had been taught.

My father continued to talk about outer space. He thought there were people living on Venus. He believed I had ruined his chances for doing something great. Something that Stoelting had secretly told him. I think he believed I was the culprit that stopped

Stoelting's important mission. I didn't argue with him. He wasn't angry or hateful and didn't complain about my mother spending money on clothes for me either. He was like a real father and talked about my future possibilities. Although I tolerated his beliefs about Stoelting, I didn't accept them. At the time, I tried to sort out what was true. I did not believe in little green men from Venus or anyplace else.

Janet still enjoyed my father's affections despite my mother's objections. Until my father's death in 1972, he believed that Janet, Stoelting and Jan were from outer space. Jan was the young woman supposedly from Venus whom Stoelting had brought to our house one evening from New York. My father insisted that Stoelting had shown him outer space secrets when he and Stoelting were in New York. I thought my father might have been drugged, but never said so.

The Catholic boarding school invited me to return for my junior year. I didn't want to return, and convinced my parents that I would do well at the local school. I was told that the principal, Mr. Singley, gave a talk to the students about my return.

At school I tried my best to fit in. Although some boys made noises like a submachine gun when I walked in the halls, I ignored them. Friends that were previously in my class were in a class ahead of me. Two girls who were my friends since 8th grade turned away when I said hello. Mary Ann Huntenburg was in my class and became my best friend. She played the title role in our school play called "Charlie's Aunt." After we graduated, she said that she didn't believe I shot anyone, because I was so good natured. She was sure I took the blame for a family member.

My high school algebra teacher was mean. He also coached the football team. He became furious if I didn't understand a math problem. This caused him to slam his book on the desk and to talk a tirade about growing up in a poor family. He said his family had searched along the railroad tracks for coal to burn. He added that some kids come from rich families and can do anything they want to do. When he said this last part, he glared at me. I surmised he believed I was bad and rich.

This upset me, but I blanked it out and remained calm. Humiliation had become familiar. On some level, I believed I deserved to be insulted and criticized. Perhaps Catholicism was partly to blame. At Our Lady of Mercy, I was told that Christ sends suffering to those He loves. I was taught that suffering is really God's love. After thinking about this for many years, I don't believe this.

Stoelting's abuse, the painful injections for gonorrhea, and how my family rejected me for years had left their mark. I stashed criticisms somewhere in the depths of my mind. I probably started doing this in grade school, from the time Lulu counseled me not to pay attention to the kids who had made fun of my buckled shoes.

I was determined to keep attending the local school and not let anything bother me. It worked. Many teachers were kind and helped me solve homework problems.

My spirit was broken in ways, but I wasn't bitter. Because I stopped standing up for myself, I did what others thought best for me. Others seemed to have my best interest in mind.

My stupid decision to let others decide for me has affected my entire life!

When I was about to graduate from high school in 1960, I applied to colleges. I was accepted into the University of Chicago and Bucknell College, now a university. I wanted to attend either one and study anthropology. My parents decided otherwise. Although my father paid for my brothers to attend college, he thought college wasn't necessary for me. My mother, who always wanted to be a nurse, thought I should be one. She met with her friend, Hazel R. who was the school guidance counselor. The two decided I should go to Kings County Hospital School of Nursing in Brooklyn, New

York. My father thought that was a great idea. He exclaimed, "We'll have a nurse in the family."

That summer, I rode my horse Woozer through the fields across from our little house. He was my last horse. That fall, I sold him for $400.

Mary Ann Huntenburg and I went on picnics and square danced at the local grange. I was eighteen and dated Mark (a pseudonym), a young man who was in the Central Intelligence Agency. He lived in a neighboring town but was stationed in Staunton, Virginia. I met him at a grange dance. He was young, handsome and soft spoken. We parked on remote country roads in his VW bus. The front seat was perfect for making out. For the first time, I experienced an orgasm.

I was furiously attracted to him. I wasn't sure whether he felt the same way toward me or if he was just out for a good time. When we parked the summer evenings were full of cricket chirps, and soft breezes cooled us after we had sex. He was always scrubbed clean, and behind his ears he smelled of a sweet scent I could never quite place. I was falling in love, but wanted some type of commitment from him to be sure he felt the same way. I was so immature, and hadn't dated at all. I had this flawed idea that if I had sex with someone, the relationship would be permanent and I'd marry them.

On one date, he asked me if I had purposely shot Stoelting. I told him of course not, but I wondered if he hadn't dated me just to find that out, since he worked for the government. This occurred to me because when my senior high school class went to Washington, D.C., that FBI agent who was at the second trial was there. That seemed to me a very unlikely coincidence.

The initial cost of the three-year nursing program was $125. I hated nursing school when I started that fall. I was terribly homesick. There were freshman hazings—nothing really terrible. Senior students came into my room at night and turned on the sink faucets. We knelt before seniors and planted imaginary flowers. We were blindfolded and supposedly taken to the morgue, but in reality we were taken to the hospital basement with many connecting tunnels. Some things were amusing. I was told that I was a piece of feces and ordered to find another student that was dubbed a bedpan. After transversing the hall several times, I found her and then took her back to the senior.

I could hardly wait for weekends, when I could take a bus or train home. My nursing routine was much like the convent's. The daily schedules, wearing uniforms and waiting for the weekend to arrive when I could escape were much the same.

Of course, I did adjust to the school's routine. Although I fared well, I was not cut out for nursing. The first time my blood was drawn, I passed out. I still pass out when I see that needle headed for my vein. I need to lie down. I have always had a weak stomach and cannot endure poop smells, or suctioning thick mucus from trache-otomies. As a nurse, it has been embarrassing to run out, while caring for a patient, so I can go throw up. Although I have these difficulties, I have persevered in caring for patients throughout the years. I've learned to smear peppermint oil under my nose to banish distasteful smells.

Nursing students at that time studied and also cared for patients on the wards. We received a stipend of $3.60 every two weeks. That paid for cigarettes, a bus trip home or pizza. A slice was fifteen cents and a pack of Benson and Hedges cigarettes cost forty nine cents. We weren't allowed to smoke in the hospital or on the grounds. I managed to smoke a pack daily after five o'clock while studying in my dormitory room. The small rooms consisted of a metal bed, desk, straight back chair, an armchair, a small sink and closet. A small dresser next to the closet kept under clothes.

All the rooms had loud wake-up buzzers. We signed a book at the reception desk for times to be awakened. The buzzing didn't stop until we pressed a large button on the wall. This informed the person assigned to the morning calls that we were awake. I often signed up to be called at several fifteen minute intervals, in case I went back to sleep. I had my bed placed so the button was right above the head of the bed, so I could just reach up and press it.

Our room doors were never locked. During the night, Miss Bamberry, a nurse, stopped by each student's room to make sure we were sleeping. She opened the door quietly and shined a flashlight about to check. If we were not in bed or had gotten up too early, our weekend pass was canceled. I didn't know this until my weekend was taken away.

One morning, I was up and dressed at six studying for an exam. Miss Bamberry came by to check. She opened the door, glanced my way and left. That Friday when I went to sign out for the weekend, there was a red line across my card indicating that I was grounded. The rationale behind this practice was to instill the belief that a nurse needed eight hours of sleep, to properly care for patients.

Students rarely lived off campus. The school was run like the army. Some of my instructors had been captains and parachute nurses in World War II. Our uniform skirts were exactly 14 inches from the floor. Our hair was worn off our collars, so it would not transfer germs to a patient.

Sanitary hand washing was branded into our brains. We never turned off a faucet with bare hands, because we were told all faucet knobs are always filthy. We always used a paper towel as a barrier to germs. We let the water run until we dried our hands with a towel then turned the knobs off with a fresh one. Doctors were trained to do the same. Patients and we were kept safe. Hand washing is still taught this way. Whether health professionals adhere to practice the technique correctly is another story.

If we had a run in a stocking, we were sent back to our room to change into a fresh one. Whatever time we took to do that was doubled, and we made it up by working on a ward the coming Friday after 5 o'clock. Time could add up, since Kings County Hospital grounds covered twenty-six square city blocks.

Our class started with 400 students and by the time graduation came only 200 were left. Most failed organic chemistry or microbiology.

Summer finally arrived and my first year in nursing was over. I returned home for vacation. Mark and I dated again and I loved him as much as ever. He had been in Brazzaville, Republic of the Congo. I had received a postcard from there. I was hopeful that I might have a future with him. His work was classified, so I never knew exactly what he did or where he was. He gave me a beautiful pearl-and-silver filigreed bracelet. Because of his work, we didn't see each other as much as I would have liked. It was often enough for me to hope for a lifetime of companionship. He never seemed critical of the way I looked or acted. I was tense when we dated and fearful that I might say or do something wrong and therefore he would cease to love me. When I was on a date, I was shy and quiet. When we parted, I missed him terribly.

Before school started that fall, my father drove me to Staunton, Virginia so I could visit Mark. We visited for a couple of hours. We held hands and walked through fields of Partridge Farm which was near the CIA compound. Crispy red and yellow leaves crunched under our steps. The sun shone upon us with a million laughing rays. We stopped and made love in the shade of a large maple tree. Oh please God make him mine, I prayed. But there were no promises of future love or marriage. I could rationalize a commitment from him was classified like his work. After all, I did have the bracelet.

My father liked him because he was planning to be a lawyer and thought he was a good match for me. I didn't have a clue how to choose a husband. I was mesmerized by Mark's manners, kindness and of course, sex.

I was back for more nursing. My second year was supposed to be easier, since I had already passed organic chemistry and microbiology. My mother cheered me on. She had wanted to be a nurse.

Occasionally I tried to talk to her about Stoelting and how I didn't want to be a nurse.

She always replied in the same way. "Let's not talk about the past. Make believe you're happy. Besides nursing is always something you can fall back on."

My father and I didn't discuss Stoelting either. He still continued seeing Janet, his secretary. If the affair had just turned into a friendship, I couldn't tell. My mother said she could sense it was not just a friendship. By now my father had stopped telling me that by shooting Stoelting, I had ruined everything. Most likely the facts brought out at the trials proving him as a conman had given my father second thoughts about Stoelting's outer space hoax.

It seemed too late for me to attend college. Since I was locked into nursing, I decided to finish the program.

My second year was more interesting. The students spent more time caring for patients and studied less didactics. We were assigned caring for obstetric and medical patients. Diseases with specific patients in mind were reviewed before an assignment. That way we could observe a patient's disease first hand. Many of our patients were severely ill since hospitals at the time had no intensive care units.

The summer before my second year, my parents had bought a house with a swimming pool in Lebanon, New Jersey. It was a charming house near a stream. I had a very cold experience during a weekend visit. My father who had suffered a recent heart attack was directed by his doctor to walk one or two miles a day to strengthen his heart. My father circumambulated the pool for exercise, while counting the number which would equal a mile.

It was the end of October. The pool was rife with dead moles and brackish water from decaying leaves and debris. While my father was walking around the pool, something lodged under his false teeth troubled him. Not wanting to stop and attend to the problem, he merely took them out and poked them into his overcoat pocket. He forgot about his teeth when he removed his handkerchief in the same pocket, to blow his nose. The teeth splashed into the black water and disappeared.

Ordinarily this would not have been a terrible predicament, except that my father had a meeting with philanthropist Laurance Rockefeller the next day. A client of my father's wanted to donate a large amount of money to the Sloan Kettering Cancer Hospital. Mr. Rockefeller was leading the fundraising for a new pavilion.

It was late in the day and the sun was beginning to set when my father rushed into the kitchen to tell the news about his teeth.

"I have to have them for tomorrow, I know about where they fell in. Maybe Alex can go in and get them," he said.

"Me? What can I do? The leaf skimmer is by the pool house." I responded.

"No no. The teeth aren't at the top, they fell down to the bottom."

"So you want me to go into the pool and get your teeth. Is that it?"

"Yes," my father said. "I'll pay you fifty dollars if you get them."

Now there was a deal. My mother had some good advice.

She said, "If you spread lard all over your body, you won't feel the cold. Swimmers crossing the English Channel do that."

I might as well try. I put on a bathing suit and larded my body.

Once outside, a slight breeze wafted over me, and indeed I didn't feel so cold. My father and mother were optimistic that I would return with the teeth–my prize.

Both my parents shined flashlights above the water as I waded down the steps toward the deep end. The water was just under my chin when my whole body became on fire from the cold. The icy water grabbed at my breath. At first I dived down with my eyes shut and tried to feel around the bottom. I could only feel silt and twigs. When I emerged and opened my eyes a dead mouse floated in front of my face. After several dives, I was ready to quit. The flashlights were no help because they illuminated a few inches of the water.

It's all right. I kept thinking, I am going to retrieve those damn teeth. Next, I carefully pushed myself down into the water at the side of the pool to feel around with my feet.

Yes, I could definitely feel the teeth. My body was still on fire with the cold. One last dive with closed eyes and groping hands at the bottom produced the teeth. Thank God!

My father and mother were relieved and I got the fifty dollars. I know I will never do anything like that again. Amazingly, I never got sick after the pool ordeal.

Chapter Sixteen

MARRIAGE

As I was leaving school for vacation, at the end of my second year in nursing, I met my future husband. I was hurrying to a family that lived in Brooklyn to catch a ride home to New Jersey. I bumped into a Chinese medical student, Yat Ting. I had encountered him a couple of months back in the hospital, when he was taking a patient's medical history. He had dated another nursing student, who was a friend. She told me she thought he was nice, but she didn't care to date a Chinese person—her mother wouldn't approve.

During my vacation, because I had earned my nursing cap, my father gave me a white convertible Ford Galaxie. It was a cream puff. The interior was blue metallic leather. I zipped around the countryside that summer with my high school friend, Mary Ann. We still went to dances at the local grange and to the beach. We were free and happy. I practiced making an occupied bed with her in it and tried to teach her just how it was done. She got wound in the sheets and we both landed on the floor. It was hilarious.

Mark and I dated happily again. He was stationed out of state. We saw a couple of movies when he was home on furlough. I recall he only came to our house for dinner once.

When I returned from vacation, Yat Ting called the dormitory and invited me out. After a couple of dates and movies, he said he loved me and wanted to marry me. I ended up writing my true love a Dear John letter.

Again, I compromised myself. Yat Ting wanted to marry me,

on the condition that I could have children. Did I agree? Yes. At the time, it seemed reasonable from his point of view. In retrospect, I was not loved for myself as a person, but as a type of brood mare. How absurd that seems now.

He said he never had sex before he dated me. He didn't like to kiss or hug in public. Sex to him was an act of self satisfaction and to make children. Despite his medical education, he held a belief that a woman could take a man's energy and that he could become sick if he had intercourse more than once every week or two. And, he knew nothing about foreplay. I rarely had an orgasm and it never occurred to him that he might think of intercourse as a loving union.

I never mentioned that I was not satisfied. I knew he didn't care, and I accepted how he was because he said it was the Chinese way. I was sexually frustrated. I discovered I could satisfy myself and didn't need a man for an orgasm. But self satisfaction was not snuggly or comforting. I made up my mind that I would never depend on a man for sexual happiness.

So, I was pregnant when I married in September. I was in my senior year of nursing school. The school didn't allow pregnant students to care for patients. After a month's rotation in psychiatry, the school found out, and I left.

Yat Ting needed a car to make house calls. He said my convertible was too showy to use. My father traded my car for a new conservative gray Ford. The car was now Yat Ting's and not mine.

Being married to a first-generation Chinese man was difficult. My mother was delighted that I had married a doctor. I put myself into being a good wife. We had moved to 169 Hester Street in New York City. The apartment had belonged to Yat Ting's father who had returned to Hong Kong. It was a fourth floor walkup apartment behind a street building. We paid $29 a month rent.

The apartment was terribly small. The bathtub was near a small sink and did double service as a table for preparing food and folding clothes. It had a porcelain-covered metal top. We took the top off to bathe. The apartment had a small green gas stove with three burners controlled by porcelain handles; we lighted it with matches. The small, tinny oven door had a turn handle.

One day, I decided to make bread. After punching down and kneading the dough, I placed it into the oven. I didn't know the apartment walls were covered with layers of painted tar paper. All the tar paper behind the stove slipped down to the floor in a long lump along the baseboard. That was the end of my baking.

I learned to cook Chinese food which I prepared in a wok. I attended The China Institute and learned to speak Cantonese. One evening, my husband dragged home a plastic gray love seat he found on the street. I did not like cheap plastic furniture, but accepted it, since we had only two old wooden chairs for seating.

Although I scrubbed the apartment and disinfected it, it was roach infested. I had never seen roaches before. They were everywhere. In all the drawers and cabinets. They were out of control. I bought a tube of phosphorous roach paste and spread it on raw potato slices, then placed them about the floor. The paste glowed in the dark, but didn't get rid of the roaches. The small silverware drawer under the sink was littered with small dark roach droppings. Yat Ting said he was given roach poop tea when he was in China. It was supposed to cure fevers. I didn't intend to drink that kind of tea.

I left a night light on near the sink to scare the roaches from the kitchen area. It didn't deter their roaming at night. I swear I could hear them marching across the metal tub cover when I was half asleep. I put all our dry food into glass containers.

Since Yat Ting was making only $45 a week as an intern, I washed my clothes and some of his in the bathtub, using a washboard. I had a pulley clothes line that stretched from my window to the front building. A concrete square between the buildings served as a playground for children and as a venue for local cat fights.

We had a skylight in the ceiling of our small water closet. The toilet was a pull-chain type with a wooden water box. One day, while on the john, I heard a noise. I looked up toward the skylight and saw a young man's face flash away. I was mortified. It never happened again, but I was afraid to put on the light at night and always went to the toilet in the dark.

In May, my first child, a son, was born. When he was about two weeks old he had a problem moving his right leg. He cried when I changed his diaper or moved his leg about. My husband immediately accused me of holding him incorrectly and was sure I had a dislocated his hip! It turned out a staphylococcus infection had settled in his knee. He had probably acquired it in the hospital. Because I was breast feeding him, the infection settled in his knee instead of spreading throughout his body. Antibiotics cured the infection. Yat Ting never apologized for accusing me.

I washed so many cloth diapers by hand, I developed carpel-tunnel syndrome. I developed a stomach ulcer from the stress of apartment living and caring for a baby. It seemed I was breast feeding and washing clothes constantly. By the time I visited my obstetrician for my six-week checkup, I was down from 150 to 118 pounds. My doctor, Shu Yuen Liu, didn't recognize me.

Yat Ting pressured me to give the pearl filigreed bracelet I got from Mark to Dr. Liu. It was the practice then not to charge fellow doctors and their families for care. Yat Ting was quite direct, saying, "We should give her a present. I want you to give her the pearl bracelet you got from that boyfriend."

The little apartment was stifling. I was cooking Chinese food, washing clothes by hand and trying to be a good mother. I was alone. My mother came from time to time to take me to my parents home in the country for a week or so. None of my classmates from nursing school came to visit me at the little apartment on Hester Street. Moreover, I was ashamed at how dingy and small it was. It reeked of oily smells from generations of Chinese cooking and herbs. I busied myself crocheting a blanket for my new baby son, but never finished because of the pain in my hands from the carpel-tunnel problem. One neurologist had told me the pain was psychological. Another doctor, Dr. Vastola who was the head of neurology for Down State Medical School diagnosed me with carpal tunnel syndrome. He prescribed a wonderful diuretic pill, Diamox. It reduced the swelling in my wrists and relieved my hand pain. I took the pill for five years. Eventually, I had to have both wrists operated on.

We moved to a larger apartment in Brooklyn, near the nursing school. I wanted to finish my senior year and become a registered nurse. My mother offered to care for my son so I could return to school in the fall. I got permission to live off-campus.

Senior year for me was my best year because I got to pick a ward for my charge nurse rotation. I learned how to admit patients, pick up orders and make assignments for the nurse aides. I wanted to get as much experience as possible. Kings County Hospital had huge medical wards, so I picked female medicine. I was the only nurse for thirty five patients.

An embarrassing experience happened one night. The huge room of the ward was encircled by patient beds and night stands. As one entered the doorway at the right, there was a bed followed by a nightstand and this continued around the room, sometimes there were two nightstands between beds. One night, one of the female patients died. We had no curtains around the beds, so we used portable screens for privacy. After she was pronounced dead by an intern, her body was carefully bathed. Her false teeth were cleaned and placed in her mouth, her jaw was tied up with long piece of muslin to the top of her head to prevent her jaw from sagging. An identification tag was tied to her right, great toe. The nurse aides and I wrapped her in a shroud cloth and placed her body on a stretcher. I transported the body to the basement morgue by the freight elevator. After my charting was done, I started dispensing the six a.m.

medications. As I approached an older patient, she exclaimed, "I can't find my teeth. Where are my teeth? They were just here."

Yikes! I had placed them in the expired woman who was now in the morgue. I hurried to the morgue and retrieved the woman's missing teeth. I cleaned those teeth in the ward utility room while my grinning nurse aides looked on. I scrubbed them with red wash, our disinfectant for beds, tooth paste and alcohol. By the time I finished, they were pristine and most likely cleaner than they had been in years.

"Where were they?" the patient asked when I returned her teeth.

"They were just outside getting cleaned," I said.

By May, I was five months pregnant again. The school doctor wanted a urine specimen from me. He routinely asked for specimens from married students to find out if they were pregnant. I knew this, and took a sample of my husband's urine instead because I wanted to finish school.

I was so thin, I didn't look pregnant, so I graduated without the school knowing I was pregnant. After I had my second child, I worked private duty at various hospitals in New York City. If my mother watched my children, I continued to work. I needed spending money.

A graduate Registered Nurse who had completed the Kings County Hospital nursing program had a wonderful education. The school was affiliated with Downstate Medical Center. Medical students, nursing students and the charge nurse of a ward made morning rounds with the interns, residents and attending doctors. The group stopped by each patient to discuss their best treatment for the best outcome. The nursing students as well as the interns were often questioned by an attending or chief resident doctor about a patient, and their differential diagnoses. The charge nurse would take notes for nursing changes. (Now a doctor must write every little change as an order to protect him or herself.) By graduation, I had specialty rotations of a month each, working through psychiatry, obstetrics and infectious diseases. I had run a ward of 35 patients for a month, when a senior. The hospital had all kinds of patients, so the experience was great. I saw a girl's leprosy rash, and sutured up a patient during an operation, because we had run out of available surgeons. But I still didn't care much for nursing.

After I graduated from Kings County Nursing School in 1964, we moved to 77 East 12th Street in Manhattan. That was when I had my second child, a cute little girl, Tsao Lin. It only took an hour for her to arrive. Actually that was too fast because she was born so fast she could not rotate her body so she came out face up! I started into labor just when my husband was coming home from working at Sydney Hillman Health Center. I arrived at the hospital the same time as my doctor. Tsao Lin was born around midnight.

Our apartment was near Union Square Park. I took my son, Ming in a stroller, and carried Tsao Lin in an "ai" on my back. An "ai" is a square piece of material about one and a half feet in diameter with long strong material straps at each corner. To use the "ai", it is placed on the bed with the straps extended. The child is placed in the center before the two lower straps are tied securely about the mother's waist. The two upper straps are drawn over the mother's shoulders and crossed at the chest, twisted and tucked in a loop under the waist straps.

I had two very nice "ais" One was thick padded silk for cool weather, the another one had nylon netting at the center to keep a baby cool. Yat Ting's aunt made these for me. I could iron clothes, cook and shop while carrying Tsao on my back this way. She didn't weigh much, so I carried her in this manner until she was about 6 months old.

I liked living near Union Square Park. Other mothers and Nannies brought children to play, especially in warm weather. Most afternoons, a Good Humor ice cream man came with his cart.

It was 1967, and I was pregnant again and due to deliver the end of June. I was packing to move again. Yat Ting bought a brownstone on twelfth street in Brooklyn. It was near Prospect Park. The brownstone had three floors. Yat Ting said he would rent out the second floor. We would occupy the street floor with a separate iron gate and the third floor with a skylight. The renters would use the wide door at the top of the entrance steps. The house had a back yard and we could get a dog.

Yat Ting's brother Joe Gua and his wife, Yee Sau (second brother's wife) and their four older children came to live on the second floor. I planted grass in the back and some roses. I had a good time living with my in-laws, Yee Sau was a great cook. She and her two daughters taught me how to prepare excellent Chinese dishes. My parents visited to see the grandchildren and eat the good food I and Yee Sau cooked. After living in the brownstone for about a year and a half, Yat Ting decided to sell it.

In 1969 Yat Ting bought a wonderful house in Flemington, New Jersey. We kept the house for about a year. I loved it. My husband came out on weekends. The three-bedroom house sat on five acres. It had a cabana and a swimming pool. I cut the grass, riding on a small tractor mower. I vacuumed the pool and swam. I had a Volkswagen square-back car and drove back and forth to my parents place for frequent dinners. I had three children, a boy, a girl and a boy and, I was pregnant with my fourth, a girl. I liked the friendly neighbors, who came to swim or drink coffee. I appreciated the country and enjoyed caring for the property. Birds were everywhere. Pheasants, rabbits and groundhogs enjoyed the place, too.

Because my husband only came out on weekends, he didn't get a chance to really enjoy the country. He had bought the house for an investment and wanted to sell it. He had purchased a co-op apartment in New York City on Gold Street that was still being built.

Before we sold the house, something exciting happened to my husband one weekend when he drove out from New York. A Chinese relative wanted a wild rabbit to cook as a tonic for her daughter who was pale and often tired. His relative believed, as many Chinese believed, that rabbit meat would increase a person's energy. As my husband drove along the rural road to our house he ran over a mysterious animal. He excitedly came into the house carrying a red furry dead fox. Having never seen a fox, he didn't know what animal it was, but he knew it was better than a rabbit.

Immediately he thought of giving it to his relative as a rabbit. I told him he shouldn't do that.

"People don't eat foxes."

"Listen to me," he said. "The Chinese say, four feet and back to the sky you can eat. Starving people in China eat rats. They eat turtles—all four feet and back to the sky."

He laid the fox on the kitchen counter. Then with a surgeon's expertise, donning latex gloves and cutting with a scalpel, he skinned and cleaned the fox. He chopped it up with a cleaver and wrapped the pieces in wax paper and carefully laid them in the freezer. He handed me the skin to salt and spread out on a garage bench.

"How can you give the fox to your relative when it's not a rabbit?" I asked.

"It's all good," he said. "A fox is even better than a rabbit. Foxes are smarter."

That Sunday, away he drove back to New York toting a new breed of rabbit that was a sure cure for tiredness.

The mother of the girl asked if he was sure that it was a rabbit, because the pieces were so large.

"Oh, yes," he replied. "The rabbits in New Jersey are huge. They're wild rabbits not like the ones you can buy in Little Italy."

The "rabbit" was cooked with Chinese herbs and red dates to make a special tonic. Presumably, the result was beneficial because the girl had more energy and eventually graduated from college.

When the New Jersey house was sold, I was back in New York, living in my husband's rented office in Chinatown. This happened because the new co-op apartment we had bought on Gold Street wasn't finished. In fact, we were all living in Yat Ting's office except my baby girl, Tzu Ling, who was born in March. My mother was caring for her in New Jersey.

My husband and I, Gay Ming, my oldest son, Tsao Lin, my oldest daughter, and Tai Ming, my second son all hid out on the second floor of number One East Broadway. The office had a small stove, but no bathtub. I washed the children and myself in a large galvanized metal tub. I filled the tub with five boiling pots of water, then added cold water. The weather was hot in the office and there was no air conditioning. The children, my husband and I slept behind a partition in the rear of the office on make-shift beds. We left the huge metal doors to a fire escape open, hoping for a breeze.

Our two older children started attending Transfiguration School, which was only two blocks away. Previously, my oldest son Ming had started at a local public school. His teacher told me that she was the only person he talked to. She said he was smart and should be in a private school. Even though my husband thought the public schools in New York City were fine, they were chaotic. Mothers fought in the lunch room and pulled off each other's stockings! I wanted my children to get the best education possible. And, it wasn't at the local public school. A good education was something that could not be taken from them.

While we stayed in my husband's medical office, I sat in the waiting area, pretending I was visiting.

Yat Ting saw no reason to rent a place to live, so I did what I could to help. I took clothes to a nearby Laundromat in a cart and returned to the office, bumping the cart up the stairs. The landlord saw me doing this. I lied and told him I was doing the laundry nearby because I was also helping my husband in the office and could kill two birds with one stone, so to speak.

The building was old and needed a thorough cleaning. Sometimes homeless people crapped in the stairwell. Weak stomach or not, I often cleaned and scrubbed the filthy steps. The hardware store owner on the first floor saw me scrubbing. He said, "If I had a wife like you, I'd put her on a pedestal."

I could never say how lonely I was. I believed I was flawed and tried to excel. I scrubbed the floors and adapted because I wanted to show Yat Ting what a good wife and mother I was. He didn't notice. He was busy building up his medical practice and figuring how to buy a building in Chinatown. We had no bank accounts in both names so I had no idea how much money there was. I begged money for the children's clothes and shoes. My mother and father often bought clothes for the children. My mother often slipped me twenty dollars. Yat Ting examined everything I bought to determine if it was worth the money. Once he told me that I needed only one pair of shoes, a black pair.

"Black goes with everything," he said.

The Gold Street apartment was a good apartment. Everything worked. It had three bedrooms, near subways and the South Street Seaport. Once in the middle of the night my daughter, Tzu Ling, had a bloody nose. She was about two years old at the time. Her father took her to the kitchen while I went to the bathroom. She came back to the bathroom and stuck her head around the door. I saw two green leaves sticking out of her nose surrounded by residual blood. Her father, although a western trained doctor, had seen people in China roll up bok tsoy leaves and stick it up the nose to stop bleeding. That's just what he did. It was too much of a shock for me, and I passed flat out onto the bathroom floor.

I wanted Ming to attend Saint Luke's School in Greenwich

Village, but he couldn't attend until the following year. My parents suggested that he could stay in New Jersey with them and attend a nearby progressive school. Ming was eager to do that and it seemed a good solution. During the year my son lived with my parents, my father died of a massive myocardial infarction. He had already suffered three heart attacks several years earlier. Being a lawyer, he loved an exciting courtroom fight and continued to try criminal cases, even though his cardiologist had advised him against doing that. After my father's funeral, my son finished out the school year while staying with my mother.

After my father's death, my husband's attitude toward me changed for the worse. He wanted me to retrieve grocery receipts to make sure I spent the money for food. He thought I could cook for less and that the children shouldn't drink so much milk.

I decided to talk to his aunt, Gru Paw, who lived in Long Island. I drove out with the children and told her about my situation with Yat Ting. After Gru Paw told Yat Ting that he should be nicer and more generous, he laughed. He said that she didn't know about money because her husband H. controlled it.

I knew Gru Paw had money. She told me, she discovered that H. was having an affair with the woman who lived across the street. He had given the woman a pearl necklace similar to one he had gifted to her, except that the woman's had a large jade piece. She was furious and told her husband that she wanted a divorce. She ranted on. He gave her $125,000 in cash and told her to go back to Hong Kong. She took the money, put it in a safe deposit box, and stayed in her house. She told me that she would go back to Hong Kong to visit, but was definitely not going to move!

Yat Ting criticized me in front of friends for the way I prepared the food. Although I generally prepared five food dishes every dinner, he often said I was lazy. He believed I was too lenient with the children. I did not believe in spanking or hitting them, but he did. He'd become furious at the slightest thing. He'd take off his slipper and run around the apartment trying to hit one of the children who had made him angry. He'd clench his teeth and raise his arm to whack my oldest son where ever he could. Once I blocked Yat Ting in the doorway of the bedroom when he raised his slippered-hand to hit one of the children. His hand was above his head as I looked into his eyes. He realized it was I, who he was about to hit, so put his hand down and did not hit me.

One evening I left with Ming, Tsao and Tai to Transfiguration Church for Ming's confirmation practice. Tzu was in a kitty coop in the bedroom with her father. When I returned, her left cheek and face were scarlet, swollen and covered with dried tears. He has slapped her so hard. He said, "She wouldn't stop crying."

When I picked her up and hugged her, she said over and over, "Sorry, sorry."

My God, I thought, What can I do?

In retrospect, I think I was close to a nervous breakdown. We had an antique portrait painting in the living room that had a witch drawn on the reverse side. It was not a portrait of a relative. I thought the drawing was creepy and decided to break up the painting and throw the damned thing out.

I had read several books about the Egyptian pyramids. "Pyramid Power" was popular. It was claimed to preserve food and keep razor blades sharp if they were placed under them. I began to make pyramid kits to sell. These had a string at the apex of the pyramid so they could be suspended. People could watch them turn. Yat Ting thought making pyramid kits was crazy. He locked me out of the bedroom. I slept in the living room on a couch. The children slept in their rooms. Yat Ting slept in the locked master bedroom.

Yat Ting wanted me to see a psychiatrist. He repeated to the children, "Your mother is crazy."

I went to a psychiatrist friend of his, Dr. W. A Chinese girlfriend went with me. I tried to explain to the doctor about pyramids and what I had read about them. He was not interested. He prescribed an antipsychotic, Mellaril. I took a pill and felt strange. That night I dreamed Yat Ting had a snake wrapped around a stick imbedded in his chest. When I told him about the dream, he locked me out of the bedroom. I explained to him, that in the movies, it is the man who sleeps on the couch, not the woman.

Yat Ting was seriously afraid of me. I asked my mother to please come and visit. I wanted her to suggest something to make matters better. She right off told my husband, that I couldn't live without love, and that she believed he didn't really love me. So the children slept in their rooms, my mother slept on the couch with me and my husband slept locked in the master bedroom.

I wanted my husband and I to go to a marriage counselor. He said I had a problem and he didn't. So I went to see an Episcopal minister, Father Vilas, who was a Jungian therapist. He also counseled nuns who were transferring to a secular life. I chatted with him, thinking I could save the marriage. I told him about the pyramid kits, how I destroyed the painting, and that I was locked out of the bedroom. I related the snake dream that made my husband afraid. I said, I thought he was afraid, too, because I was fascinated with Egypt. The pyramids and the snake dream freaked my husband out.

I told the therapist how my husband continually told the children I was crazy. He listened to me for what seemed hours. When the therapist asked about finances, I said I had no idea how much money my husband made, because we had no joint bank accounts. I told Father Vilas that I showed all my grocery receipts to Yat Ting because he wanted to make sure I spent the food money on food.

Finally, he turned and said, "You don't have a marriage to hold together. There are no bank accounts in your name, you are isolated and undermined as an individual."

He pointed out that a caduceus is comprised of two snakes not one.

He then took a dollar bill from his pocket and showed me the pyramid with the eye of Horus at the top – the all-seeing eye. He said the pyramid was a sign of completeness as was a square in Jungian theory. I asked him if he thought I was crazy. "No," he said.

He added, "You see the problems in your marriage very well."

He referred me to Ross L. Hainline, M.D., who at the time, headed the Jungian Institute in New York. Dr. Hainline told me I saw my situation very well, that I was not crazy and added that he held many degrees and offered to testify in court in my behalf. He advised me not to go to a psychiatrist or doctor that was recommended by Yat Ting or to take any medicines prescribed by them.

I wasn't too keen on divorce just yet. Divorcees in my family were frowned upon. Divorced people were tainted in society's eyes.

Little by little, over the next few weeks, more difficulties built up in the marriage. After twelve years, I felt the differences over money, the education of our four children, and my husband's ideas of my role as a wife were irreparable. We divorced.

At the time, all the children were attending St. Lukes grammar school in Greenwich Village. My youngest daughter, Tzu Ling, was in kindergarten. Including child support, Yat Ting agreed to pay for the children's private schooling through high school. I thought if they had that, it would at least give them an opportunity to attend a good college. Looking back, my decision to get a divorce was brave. I accepted less alimony in return for my children's education. My husband had his money tied up in a corporation and reported about twenty five thousand dollars a year income. His rent from his Grand Street building and a parking lot on Hester Street plus his medical practice income were in a corporation.

I was shocked recently when I found out that Yat Ting had his psychiatrist friend, Dr. W. write a letter in the 1970's stating that I was deranged and an unfit mother. He showed it to my son a couple of years ago. I didn't know he had such a letter written, and why would he show such a thing to my son after all these years? I'm so glad I got a divorce.

In retrospect, I think Yat Ting would have had a better marriage if he had married a Chinese woman. He had come to the United States from a poor family in Canton, China, where he had gone without food and clothing. When he was a young boy, his mother had died of cholera during a flood. His father had remarried a woman who hated Yat Ting. Because of her meanness and jealousy he went to live with his brother and his sister-in-law. His two older brothers and other relatives came to the U.S. and then sponsored Yat Ting to come. When he arrived he was already in his twenties. He finished high school and went on to City College of New York. He had to scrimp money along the way and shared a tenement apartment on Orchard Street in New York City. Throughout his life before I met him, he was living on the edge of severe poverty.

This harsh background laid the groundwork for his financial insecurity. We were mismatched from the beginning. I tried being as Chinese as possible, but it wasn't enough. He didn't trust me and couldn't love me. I don't think he can trust anyone, except perhaps one of his children. At the time of our divorce he had bought a large factory building and a parking lot and was making quite a lot of money from his medical practice. His harsh poverty stricken past made it difficult to share or trust people with his money. I could not live with distrust. I needed love and acceptance.

Chapter Seventeen

A SECOND TRY

I met my second husband, Frank Pallizo (a pseudonym), at a Unitarian church social. I dated him for five years because I wanted to make sure the marriage would "take." He was divorced and had three children. The two of us and our children went tent camping in the Adirondack Mountains. We traveled on hot summer days to Long Island beaches to swim. I wasn't thrilled that Frank liked to hunt, especially deer. I could put that aside because he had other things going for him. The children and he got along and he liked to fish and showed them how to do that. We also went deep sea fishing.

According to the divorce agreement, Yat Ting had custody of the children every other weekend. He had difficulty managing all four and frequently didn't include our daughter Tsao Lin, my second child. He said she didn't obey him. It had been apparent to me that he favored boys more than girls. When Tsao Lin was in fifth grade, my husband refused to include her on a two week vacation with her brothers and sister.

My brother, Tony, in Arizona heard about her exclusion and invited her to vacation at his ranch for two weeks so she would have a vacation too. She rode his horse and got a taste of the West. My mother also sent Tsao Lin and me on a trip to Hawaii so she wouldn't feel left out. Her father's actions did not make her feel loved. I tried to make good out of the bad. I did let her go on a class trip to Egypt with her seventh grade class. She had an experience of a lifetime, that other children could never have had.

After my divorce from Yat Ting, I needed more money to care for the children. I went back to court to prove that the cost of food, clothing and school supplies had risen dramatically. Our fights were always about money. I was annoyed because he made me pick up the child support check at his office–he refused to mail it. He said he was afraid it would be lost in the mail. His apartment was one block away from mine on Gold street. He wanted me to pick the checks up there. I couldn't stand to look at him. The many griefs of the marriage would sting my mind like tacks thrown against silk. I frequently asked my son, Ming, to get the monthly checks from his father. It was a callous thing to do because my son had to listen to his father's tirade about me while he wrote out the check. Although I have apologized to my son, who is now an adult, I still cringe at my cowardice. I was off the radar how the divorce affected my children.

I thank God that my ex-husband agreed to pay for their private high school educations.

Although Yat Ting agreed to pay for them, my youngest daughter, Tzu Ling, traded going to Stuyvesant High School in lieu of a private high school. Her father told her he would pay for college. It didn't happen. He had gone to City College of New York and did not want to pay for Columbia University. Scholarships and friends' loans made it possible for her to attend. Eventually she graduated from Columbia Medical School. When she graduated as a medical doctor, she owed about three hundred thousand dollars. Ironically her father paid for my younger son Tai Ming, to attend Columbia University for a masters degree in architecture.

My oldest son, Ming, graduated from New Mexico Technological Institute. He managed to get through on his own. He now has a doctorate in chemistry.

Tsao Lin my oldest daughter graduated from Fashion Institute of Technology and later from acupuncture school where she studied herbal remedies. She's presently on The New York Acupuncture

Board. When she was accepted into the United Nations School for high school, the school didn't call me to inform me when she should start. I called and a woman in the office told me that a man had called informing the school that my daughter was not going to attend, that she was going to attend Brooklyn Technological School instead.

When I called Yat Ting about this he said, "I didn't do that. Someone else must have."

I told the United Nations School that she indeed was going. The school personnel scrambled to inform the student who had taken her place that there had been a change. Although I was divorced, I was constantly alert to how Yat Ting might pull a fast one. If there was something the children needed and I asked him for money he gave excuses not to help. He'd say, "Ask your mother, she has money." I tried not to ask him. We had different ideas about money and our children's needs.

I dated Frank for several months before he moved into my apartment. We had things in common. We continued trips to museums and picnics at the beaches with the children. My mother liked him and enjoyed his company when we visited her in New Jersey. Although I waited five years before getting married to him, the marriage lasted only for about three years.

My new love of art tore it apart. Tzu Ling, my youngest daughter wanted to attend The Art Students League with a school-mate. I didn't want her to go by herself, so I enrolled in Isaac Soyer's painting class which was scheduled at the same time.

I had continued to sketch for years after studying art in the convent. I first started painting when I was about five years old. Then, I used watered food coloring for paint and a discarded wing feather from Peepsie, our canary, as a brush.

At art school, I was hot. I could paint well.

Mr. Soyer said, "You've studied a lot of art."

I said, "No, only one class in high school."

I had taken one art class at the convent school. I did learn about colors and their compliments. I was delighted to paint. I had money to attend school because my mother had given me her house in New Jersey which I sold after she went to live in a nursing home.

It was 1981 and the money from the sale of the house gave me the freedom I needed. I took day and afternoon classes at The Art Students League and an evening class for a short time at the National Academy. I became class monitor for Dan Dickerson's painting class at the league and did not have to pay tuition. I began to win prizes. A painting was accepted into a juried museum show and I sold a painting to a Boston art collector.

Frank was jealous. I wish he could have been my fan. I was stunned when a fellow art student told me her husband built a studio over their garage so she could paint. He loved her.

Before I met Frank, he had been an art director in an advertising agency and had lost his job. After his stint in advertising, he became a security guard at a large hospital. He was working as a guard when I met him with aspirations of changing to a more meaningful job. He hated the security job but continued working for the benefits and salary because they paid for child support.

I loved to paint, but he couldn't endure it. He didn't allow me to hang my paintings on the apartment walls. He couldn't bear my creative spirit. My hungry eyes gobbled up so many subjects to paint.

I rented a studio on 14th Street that I shared with artists from the league. We each paid $25 a month. After dinner with the children and Frank, I sped off to paint at the studio. I often took our dog for company. I got a portrait commission from a former Cuban dancer who left Cuba before Castro came to power. I painted her at the 14th Street studio.

I was seeing a psychotherapist, Dr. Carol Dilling. She commissioned me to paint a group of masks for her waiting room. I got busy painting masks from Upper Volta, Dogon, New Hebrides, Alaska, and New Guinea. It happened that my husband's therapist shared a waiting room with Dr. Dilling.

Frank got closer to his therapist as I got closer to my art. His therapist told Frank what he and his son did together such as kayaking, camping, and what movies they saw. I found out more about Frank's therapist than I could have imagined.

I had been practicing Transcendental Meditation for several years. I thought my husband might try it. Frank's therapist told him meditation was mind masturbation.

My husband began consulting his therapist before we made decisions. These were not major decisions, but where to go on vacation and things like that. He would not discuss the subject with me.

Instead he'd say, "I can't discuss it now, I want to run it by V. first."

He said his therapist was like a good brother. I perceived him as a wedge between Frank and me. I set up a meeting with his therapist and challenged him about Frank. I wanted to know why the therapist had never explored how Frank might change his job, and why he often said that he would never see the light at the end of the tunnel, meaning his job. His therapist said Frank wasn't ready for a change.

I thought marriage counseling might renew our love and communication. We attended The Ackerman Institute for Family Therapy. I wasn't sure if it was working. Now my husband talked to his therapist about our meetings at Ackerman.

During a session at Ackerman, I said, "I don't even talk about art."

Frank said, "You don't, you live it. I can't get away from it. I go to see my therapist and your paintings are on the wall."

My artist friends thought this was the best complement any artist could get. I thought so too.

So, I ended the marriage although art wasn't the only problem. I would not give up my art for anyone. It was the expression of my very soul.

The decision to get a divorce came about during a session at Ackerman.

Frank asked, "Is this marriage counseling or divorce counseling?"

The therapist P. said, "What is it, Alex?"

I said, "I want a divorce."

Frank got angry during the session. I felt it was my fault that the marriage didn't continue. But, I had grown and saw the world in a different light. His enthusiasm for the museums and art had vanished and I had caught it like a disease.

After Frank and I went home that night, Frank took some blankets and pillows from the bedroom and slept on the couch in the living room. He moved out the next day.

I've worked as a nurse most of my life to make ends meet. However, I have painted regularly since I began taking classes.

I continued therapy with Dr. Dilling for several years. Initially I went to her because I had slapped my oldest daughter when she was 12 years old. The two of us had screaming battles about the chores I assigned to her. I was concerned about her escalating anger toward me and my own temper. My four children had chores such as grocery shopping and cleaning. I had a weekly rotating schedule.

I learned from Dr. Dilling that it was normal for girls to fight with their mothers. By confrontation, a daughter could integrate into her personality what she liked about her mother and reject what she didn't. Dr. Dilling told me that it was okay for my daughter to complain and even call me names as long as she did what I had asked her to do. She said that I shouldn't expect her not to complain. This was a process of individuation.

As I continued therapy, I began talking about myself. My daughter wasn't such a problem anymore. I talked about work, covered why I got divorced and how I didn't like to argue about money or beg for it.

One day Dr. Dilling asked me, "What happened to you when you were around the age of your daughter?"

"Twelve?" I asked.

"Yes," she answered.

At the time, I couldn't remember much. During two more years of weekly therapy, I managed to tell her snippets about Stoelting and his wife. I recalled small parts of painful memories. I called them flash memories. A flash memory was one on the verge of remembering the whole of it but gone when I tried to speak about it. More of it comes to the surface over time until it is all displayed.

I related memories about Stoelting, my family and the convent school. Therapy was depressing. After a session, I would often treat myself to a chocolate ice cream cone and savor the taste as I walked to the subway to head home.

It occurred to me that Dr. Dilling might "catch" the terribleness of my past if I related my horrible experiences to her. She assured me that she could not catch suffering. The memories of Stoelting were emerging bit by bit. Dr. Dilling would listen and nod during sessions.

After two years of therapy, during a session, she lurched up in her chair, wide-eyed, "So this is what you're talking about! This man Stettling raped you!"

I asked, "Do you mean after two years, you didn't know what I was talking about?"

She explained that I spoke of things that were not coherent to her nor in a logical sequence. I was amazed at this revelation.

Since the time I started therapy, I have painted images of my abusive past. I call the collection the perpetrator series. Images in the paintings are jammed together. One part becomes another. The belly of an airplane is also a coffin. A dog's nose is superimposed as a black shoe of a clown doll that's being dragged along by a little girl.

I do not explain the paintings. Sometimes viewers become upset while others think them hilarious. One woman called me, saying that a painting upset her for three days. She said the painting should not be exhibited. I told her, if the painting upset her for three days, it was a damned good painting.

Chapter Eighteen

FRANCE –
POUR LE SOUVENIR

After my second divorce I went landscape

painting in France. Beth W. who was a classmate of mine at the Art Students League, generously invited me to stay a couple of weeks at her country house in the Ardeche area. Her house sat on the side of a mountain outside the small town of Laroche. Beth had installed a flush toilet. This was a curiosity to the locals because toilets were a luxury. Most people had privies.

Beth's garden was filled with vegetables and pear trees resembling illustrations from fairytale books. Chestnut trees at the back of the house gave ample shade for painting. A small attached room that Beth used for guests had once been used for roasting chestnuts.

The cool mountain air fragrance elicited happy memories from my childhood. Pale sunshine on the deep green-blue mountains was exhilarating. According to local lore, an ancient mountain road across a valley, at the front of the house, had been used by Druids. Once at her house, the world seemed to me as it should be. I was happy and free. France felt like I had come home.

Beth also had also invited two young women to paint. We all left to paint in the morning and returned at lunchtime to eat and drink wine, before going out again with our easels and canvases.

Stone paths built in Roman times led from one village to another. A government path tender kept the paths free of weeds. I could easily venture to the nearest village to paint. One day we drove in Beth's small Renault to paint a field of golden hay, similar to what Van Gogh might have painted. Towns with ancient cobblestone streets were scattered throughout the area.

The best pizza I ever ate was in a small, French, mountain cafe. The fresh thin-crusted, tomato-basil pizza with a lattice pastry top was superb. I believe the best ice cream was and is in France also. Perhaps the food tasted so good because I was having an affair.

I had briefly attended the French Institute before my trip. I spoke a little French, but I wanted to speak more fluently. I learned French much faster with the help of a lover. It was August and fete time. A time to celebrate the Catholic saints. Every few days, a town had a fete or festival to celebrate a saint's birthday. There was music, wine, food and dancing. Large tables were set up at the edge of a square, often on bare dirt. People ate homemade sausages and locally made food, drank wine, chatted and danced the lambada on the dirt. At one fete, a very handsome disc jockey eyed me and kept smiling. I thought he was enchanting. He approached Beth saying in French that he wanted to take me out. Beth nodded in agreement. After the music was over and he had packed his equipment, he came to the table where I was waiting.

The two of us walked down dimly lighted streets past churches and sat in a park. For the longest time, we just held hands. The easy flow of his French mesmerized me, although I often didn't have a clue as to what he meant. We walked and stopped like this until early morning, when eventually we kissed and kissed. We loved our way into a small hotel in a nearby town. We were exhilarated.

For my whole life, I so wanted to be loved. He was attentive. That morning he sang arias from Tosca to me before he returned me to the house.

A few days later, he brought a crate of peaches for all of us painters. He took delight in the smallest things I did, how I put on my stockings or how I applied my lipstick. He was smitten. All this attention was new and exciting. I couldn't get enough of him or France.

He drove me to the Ardeche region to see a tremendous glacial boulder. We picnicked in the mountains and made love on a grassy slope under a dazzling moonlit sky. Incredibly energized, I was painting more than ever.

A charming widower from Belgium was attracted to me, too. He had spent most of his life in South Africa. He was older than I. His wife had died a short time before I met him. Because she had been bedridden and too ill to attend concerts, he had a quartet in to play for her at their home. The house had been an old mill before it was transformed into a beautiful villa. It had a large swimming pool that edged out above the Vals River. This man was charming, too.

When I returned to New York, he sent beautiful handkerchiefs and love letters to me via Beth. I was still not ready to settle down or live in France. I thought living in France with him might rob me of my newfound freedom. In retrospect, I was too immature to see the possibilities that had been laid before me by such a kind person.

The disc jockey said he would wait six years for me to return, but no longer. I missed him terribly at first when I returned to New York, but knew he was my liaison souvenir.

The French know how to enjoy life. Shops close from noon to 2 p.m. All business is halted except for cafes and restaurants which close from 3 to 5 p.m. People relax. Some return home to lunch, to nap or just to visit. People take a leisurely lunch and drink wine. When they return to work, they bustle about rejuvenated. I found the French enjoy gossiping and political talk.

People I met asked me many questions about New York and how crime was controlled. What did I think of our then mayor and were our taxes high? They were curious about people and their ideas. The French I met were veritable knowledge vacuums. They subscribe to love. Love in and of itself is erotic. I found they believe relationships should be honored and nurtured. The people in the small village of Laroche had an efficient way of correcting violations of local social norms. If a person acted in a despicable way, he or she was boycotted.

Paul, an older man, had treated his girlfriend, Jeanine, badly when he was drunk. Jeanine had left for Paris. The townspeople put out the word not to visit Paul until he realized he shouldn't have disrespected her. I never found out what Paul's transgression was, but when he invited us to stop for a glass of wine, we said, "Not now, Paul, we're very busy." All his neighbors avoided him. They meant to shame and punish him. Eventually they stopped after Paul understood their disapproval of his actions.

Returning to New York was difficult. I would have stayed in France if I could have, but I had to return to work. As I boarded the Air France plane for home, the flight attendant gleefully saw my French easel and was delighted to find I was a painter. She immediately stopped me from storing the easel in one of the large bins at the rear of the plane. Instead, she placed it in back of the first class section. This made it extremely easy for me to disembark. I will never forget her kindness. I had been exhausted after searching for my plane in the huge Paris airport. The French food and wine served on the plane weren't bad either.

Chapter Nineteen

THIRD MARRIAGE

After two marriages that didn't work out, I married again! As I was descending the steps of the City Hall subway, I ran into Alan (a pseudonym). He was an artist. I first met him when he was substituting at the league. His father, also an artist, had died. Alan shared a small apartment in midtown with his mother. He was animated and delighted to see me again. He had been teaching a class at a Brooklyn art school. When we met, I had been working at Salomon Brothers, in their medical department, and managed to paint at home after work. Later that week he invited me to lunch. He was rotund and enjoyed lots of good food. We began dating and frequented the best restaurants in New York. Greek onion soup with gobs of cheese at the bottom of the bowl was his favorite. We had art in common and visited museums throughout the city. I thought I had found my match.

Alan proposed marriage and I accepted. We had perhaps only dated for a couple of months. I decided that we should marry at The Pen and Brush. It was an exclusive woman's club of which I was a member. My former art teacher, Dan Dickerson would "give me away." My daughter, Tsao, made a beautiful off-white dress for me. Invitations were sent out to my family and friends. I hired a judge to officiate and a piano player. Plans were going well until a day or two before the wedding.

As Alan and I were walking down a Manhattan street, he asked, "Don't you want to know what Melissa thinks?"

"Who is Melissa?" I said.

He said, "Melissa is one of my alter-egos."

"What are your alter-egos?" I asked

"Well, I have many parts of my personality." He said.

"How many parts do you have?" I asked.

"Oh, about seven, and they must have their opinions heard. But most of them really like you."

He named male and female names and told me which ones were the most demanding.

Well, that was a new twist to our relationship. All the time we had been dating, there had been many parts of Alan's personality that had been judging me—telling him whether they agreed with me or not.

"So they talk to you and tell you what they think?' I asked.

"Yes, they do. I hope this doesn't upset you. Nothing has really changed between us."

The wedding was planned, but the relationship had certainly changed.

There was a moment just before I was to be married that I thought, don't do this. But I did. In retrospect, I should have said "I'm not getting married. Let's have a party." I was saving face and I thought it would have been bad form to do that.

We honeymooned for a week in Rhinebeck, New York. I was alarmed and nervous the entire time, because I didn't know just which part of Alan was present. He had changed into something scary.

When we returned to the city, we went to the Ackerman Institute for counseling, the same place that Frank and I had gone.

The therapist asked Alan if she could hear what Melissa thought. A high pitched woman's voice came from Alan. I realized then, that I could not live with a person whose mind was fragmented in that way. The marriage had lasted two months. Alan couldn't understand why I was divorcing him. He met with my lawyer several times and said the divorce was a huge mistake.

I blamed myself for his disappointment because I did marry him after he told me about the many personalities. This had led him to think that our relationship was okay. I know some people's multiple personalities can be integrated. Alan seemed to have enjoyed several of his—he was never alone. I believe certain ones were comforting and entertained him in ways unbeknown to me.

I do know that I was still trying desperately to find love so my life would be happier. I thought that was the key that would unlock my feeling of emotional stains. I was always looking for love and validation.

There was one final marriage, a fourth. In retrospect, I am embarrassed about my marriages because, I now realize that my choice of men did not remedy what I thought I lacked or make me complete.

Chapter Twenty

CURED OF MARRIAGE FOREVER

By 1991 my children had left the apartment on Gold Street in New York City. Gay Ming, my oldest son, was living in New Mexico. My daughters, Tsao Lin and Tzu Ling, were sharing an apartment in the city. Tai Ming, my third son, was living in a loft on Grand Street. It was in the factory building owned by his father.

In the spring and summer of 1991, I was working in New York City with the homeless mentally ill through a Boston University grant. The university's research had demonstrated that homeless mentally ill people could be helped by a communication technique. I and others were trained in that type of communication. Although we were not allowed to label them, most of our clients were schizophrenics. I enjoyed my job. The philosophy of the program honored the clients' choices to refuse medication and to live on the streets. I traveled throughout the city and helped clients obtain housing, medical care and other services. Sometimes my client didn't show up on a certain day, but later came to our center for help. These were people who didn't know where the soup kitchens were and who ate from garbage containers. Some had not had their clothes and shoes off for months. Some could not be helped.

One beautiful clear summer day I had just finished cleaning my apartment on Gold Street. I was hot and tired but not yet ready to bathe, so I went to cool off on a bench near the South Street Seaport. I was happy because my cleaning was done. A salty cool breeze soothed my hot face. I must have sat for some time before a handsome man in his thirties approached.

"Why are you just sitting here?" he asked.

"I am resting," I said.

He sat on an adjacent chair and proceeded to tell me about himself. He seemed delightful. He was from the Middle East but spoke English quite well. He said he had always wanted to come to New York and see the culture. He said that his mother suffered from a mental condition and added that he was trying to find a job to help support her and pay for her medical care. We sat and talked for a couple of hours. He was clean-shaven, handsome and eighteen years my junior. He asked if we could go for coffee. He had been working in a restaurant in Brooklyn. Aslan (a pseudonym) had a green card, but was not a citizen.

We sat in a small shop on Fulton Street, drank coffee and talked. That was the beginning of a serious relationship. We bicycled and picnicked on weekends, took long walks in Central Park and picked flowers along the way.

He was a good lover and said he loved me more that anyone he had ever dated. However, he lamented that if he could only become a citizen, he could then help his poor mother. He wanted me to marry him, so he could become a citizen.

He begged to move in with me. He said that he had been living with an American family and shared a room with their son, but that the father didn't want him to stay any longer. I let Aslan move in. He brought his clothes and a bicycle. One morning while he was shaving, with lather on his face, he turned and said, "Honey, I just want to be married so I can help my mother." He seemed genuinely morose. I was overwhelmed with sorrow for his situation. He had lost his job. He said the restaurant didn't have enough business. I had faith that he did want to work and would probably find another job. I wanted to help him in any way I could and I wanted desperately to be loved.

I began to give him money to send abroad for his mother.

She ran water constantly in her apartment and had no money for the water bill. I sent money for that. She needed money for food and clothing, too. I did marry him. He was attentive, but didn't work.

After I had worked for several months with the homeless, Aslan wanted me to work elsewhere because he didn't like the fact that I was paired with a man to go out on the streets to help the clients. He didn't say he was jealous. He said he didn't like the idea that I was working with several men. I then changed my job to a nursing director at a drug rehab in the Bronx, New York.

I supported him and his family for five years, using the sale money from my mother's house. I later discovered Aslan secretly used the money I had given him for his mother to buy an apartment for himself which was a floor above hers. One winter, I traveled to Aslan's home in Turkey. Of course, I paid for the flights on Turkish Airlines and other expenses.

When we arrived, we stayed a few days in Istanbul. We toured the underground Grand Bazaar and other parts of the city. I wore a burka to avoid the aggressive salespeople who would have otherwise concluded that I was a tourist.

Because soft coal was used for heating, the air in the city was thick with gray smoke. One morning three men were walking their bears. The brown bears had collars and chain leads. They seemed tame enough and I asked to pet one. As I was petting its head, Aslan took my picture. The men wanted money for the photo. Aslan argued with the men in Turkish and turned away. He said to me, "We're not paying them anything because they're Kurds. We then walked around the city and took pictures. I visited several mosques, Hagia Sophia which is now a museum and a museum for Suleiman The Magnificent. One particularly beautiful item was a jeweled horse bridle set with rubies.

It was Christmastime and it began to snow. Only one shop had a small Christmas tree in the window. Knowing that people back in the states were celebrating the holiday, I wished I was back home. I felt very lonely because I did not speak the language and few people spoke English.

Aslan and I took a four hour bus ride south to his home. I saw that indeed his mother did have a mental problem. Her two bedroom apartment was adequate, but she ran the water in the apartment constantly. Aslan had a sister and brother-in-law. The three of them sought a psychiatrist to make a house call to treat his mother. The doctor came but, when the doctor tried to give her an injection, the mother became hysterical. Aslan and his sister decided that she shouldn't get the injection after all. While the psychiatrist was still at the apartment, Aslan's sister wanted one of my art postcards. The card had a portrait of a dog and my New York telephone number on it. I handed the card to her. Aslan quickly snatched the card, grabbed a pair of scissors and cut off the phone number. The doctor asked me why Aslan did this. I said that he didn't want anyone to call us in New York. It was really a paranoid response but I didn't say that in front of Aslan and his relatives.

We stayed a month. Aslan took me about the neighborhood and introduced me as a doctor. I did not know the Turkish word for nurse. But when I heard him say the word doctor and gesture towards me, I shook my head and said, "No, a nurse." Aslan had low self esteem and other mental quirks such as paranoia that had not registered before. He would not allow me to go out alone for a walk. He was always with me. Winter in Turkey was cold and dreary. I prayed to Allah five times a day like everyone else because I did not want to disrespect or irritate his mother or others.

In retrospect, I believe when Americans meet people from another country, their peculiarities are taken as cultural differences. This may or may not be true.

When we returned to New York I returned to work as direc-tor at Project Return, the drug rehab center in the Bronx. Aslan never could find a job. I helped him apply for various jobs and found advertisements for work he might like. He claimed he applied for work, but wanted to get a job as a television actor. That was fanciful.

During the fourth year of our marriage, Aslan became horribly nervous and controlling. When we were shopping, he accused me of looking into men's eyes. He said this meant that I wanted to have sex with them. He studied my expressions to check whether I did this. He marched back in forth in the living room while humming for no apparent reason. Then he'd accuse me of searching his pant pockets or some other ridiculous thing. I defended myself and wondered why he had changed and ceased to be loving. He became extremely paranoid. He accused me of controlling his mind when I was asleep. I'd awaken in the night to find him staring at me. He'd be peering down at me with his face about six inches above mine. I would be startled awake and would demand, "Aslan, what are you doing?"

He'd answer, "I'm looking at you because you're so beautiful."

"Go to sleep," I'd say.

He'd turn over on his side pretending to sleep. Later in the night, I'd awake and he'd be right in my face again.

He accused me of bizarre things. He said, "You felt my arm last night to see if it was broken. I know you're sleeping with some people at the drug rehab." (I was the nursing director at the time).

He said shocking things to me such as, "You want behind sex," and, "You married me because I am younger."

I became sleep deprived and hyper-vigilant because of Aslan's actions. I was frustrated and stressed because my responses to his accusations had no effect. Work became a relief. I looked forward to being away from him. This continued for over a month. It seemed much longer because I was dumbed from lack of sleep and not knowing what Aslan might do.

I had suggested he see a psychiatrist. He did supposedly see one. When he returned, he told me that the doctor gave him some pills for sleeping. He said he really got them for me and wanted me to take them. Of course, I didn't.

I loved him dearly, and wanted him to be free of his paranoia. I wanted him to be like he was when we met. In the beginning, we were happy. We rode bicycles throughout New York City and on Long Island. We drove out to New Jersey and cycled over the river to New Hope, Pennsylvania and visited antique shops. Aslan cooked and cleaned tirelessly. He had been overjoyed to see me when I returned from work. I rationalized that other women had relationships like mine, where the wife worked and the husband kept house and cooked.

Now our relationship was dissolving. I could no longer trust him. I couldn't clearly grasp what was so wrong. I began listing his escalating angry accusations and odd behavior:

1. He told me I'm old now, and he didn't like that Stoelting had sex with me when I was young.

2. He made collages of me with sexual overtones and sent them to my friends.

3. He told his friends that I had sex with a fellow artist.

4. He berated me about not getting my art into a gallery in SoHo. He said, "You didn't talk good enough."

5. He said, "I saw you in my mind when I was visiting my mother." Then he accused me of having an affair with my former art teacher.

6. He accused me of being jealous and that I didn't want him to be successful with his art— the collages he began making after we were married.

7. He was angry that my ex-husband got some money through the divorce.

8. He said I should have gotten my life together by now and therefore should have lots of money—that he needs.

9. He was angry because I said a young man I saw was handsome.

10. "Yes, I know something. When I was away you went on a vacation."

11. He was angry at my son-in-law, claiming he is lazy. "Yes, I know"

12. He phoned a girl friend of mine and asked her if I was having an affair with someone.

13. He was angry that I had friends over for dinner when he was visiting his native country.

14. He was angry that my son had looked at his collages. He said that my son would copy them and be successful and that he wouldn't.

15. He was angry that he gave two of his collages to an artist I knew in New Jersey.

16. He was angry that I didn't write a good letter to try and get his work into a gallery.

17. He was angry that my children might get something from my death!

18. He did not want me to talk on the phone.

19. He was afraid that if he went out of the country, someone I knew might be able to stop the plane and he wouldn't be able to return.

20. He would not let me go out by myself even to the store. He was afraid I would throw him out and he would be out on the street, (since I was a director of drug rehab).

21. He said he had strange feelings on Thursday. Said something would happen on Thursdays.

In reviewing my notes, it is apparent now that he was severely paranoid. I hope this list may be beneficial for others in similar situations. It was not safe for me to be with him, but it's hard to see the picture when you're in the frame. He became increasingly angry and fearful as the above list demonstrates.

I could not clearly understand at the time how toxic my relationship with Aslan had become. I tried to appease him, thinking he would get better. More happenings helped me make up my mind to release him.

Aslan accompanied me to a friend's house where I was to perform Therapeutic Touch on a man who had suffered a recent stroke.

Therapeutic Touch is a method of energy transference developed by Dolores Krieger and Dora Kunz whereby a practitioner's hands are moved over the patient's body without touching them. This allows healing energy to transfer from a healthy practitioner to an ill person, often with beneficial results. I had learned this practice when I was nursing at a major New York City hospital. At that time a study was made on heart surgery patients which proved the practice beneficial.

I told Aslan I needed to be alone with the man so I could concentrate on trying to help him. I worked on the stroke victim for about twenty minutes. As I emerged from the room, Aslan was sitting next to the man's wife. He jumped up and spoke nonsense.

"What were you doing in there? You were doing something! I know," he said.

He launched a tirade of accusations that shocked my friends. I apologized and left with him.

On the trip home, Aslan's palms sweated. He held out his wet palms for me to see before rubbing them on his pants.

He said, "I don't want you to do anything like that again."

I nodded in agreement. He was seized by a weird fear. He wouldn't tell me what.

I was mortified by what had happened in front of my friends. After we got home he wanted to have sex. I decided I was never going to have sex with him again. I was no longer attracted but feared him instead.

He pleaded to have sex and said, "I need it. A man has to have sex."

My decision was firm.

"I don't feel in the mood." I told him. "Sex is not something you can turn on and off like a T.V."

Again that night, I couldn't sleep. Finally Aslan accepted that he was not going to have sex with me, but he peeped and stared in my face whenever I turned to see what he was doing.

I told, H. a psychiatrist with whom I worked, at the drug rehab what Aslan was doing. I told him that I had not slept for weeks because Aslan watched me throughout the night and probably slept during the day. I said I was terrorized when we were together and that my relationship with him got more hellish day by day.

A few days later, H. came into my office.

He said, "This is not therapy. This is advice. You are not safe. Your life is in grave danger! This man is paranoid and you definitely are not safe if you stay with him."

I was unnerved. Old fears of Stoelting surfaced. I knew deep down my life was threatened.

I asked the doctor how I could get Aslan to leave.

"The next time your husband accuses you of something, you should tell him that you are very angry. Perhaps even throw some pillows around and ask him to leave," He assured me that Aslan would leave if I did something like this.

"What I should do with his belongings." I asked.

He said, "Put it all in storage and mail him the key."

One afternoon, I had the opportunity to change my dreadful life and cause Aslan to leave. I had awakened from a nap and walked into the kitchen. Aslan glared at me.

He said, "I know you are psychic and you were in my brain trying to control me when you were in the bedroom. I know you feel my arm at night to see if it is broken."

I didn't even answer to these accusations. If there was ever a time to get him to leave, this was it.

I said, "Aslan, I am very angry and I don't know what I might do. I am really angry!"

He looked at me in amazement, "Really?"

"Yes, I don't know what I might do," I repeated.

I sat on the living room couch and acted as angrily as I could, and said, "I'm so angry, I don't know what might happen. You have to leave!"

"Okay," he said.

He rushed into the bedroom. After a short time, he emerged carrying a canvas gym bag. He had packed his clothes.

Staring nervously, he asked, "Where should I go?"

"You might stay at the YMCA," I told him. I gave him some money and he promptly left.

I was shaken by what had just happened but relieved. That evening, I called a locksmith and had the apartment lock changed. For the first time in perhaps months, I slept soundly.

The psychiatrist at work was a true friend. I told him what had transpired and that he was right about the threat to my safety. The peace that I had when Aslan left was short lived and did not return for another year.

From that February in 1995 until 1996, I was stalked and harassed by him. Time after time, week after week, he would pop up. "Hi sweetie, I am just here, too."

Then he'd approach and grab my arm and ask for a kiss. He phoned my friends, children and brothers slandering me. He told them I was having sex with people where I worked. One friend later told me that Aslan told her such a sob story, she believed the things he said against me. She ended up having sex with him.

Another friend called me asking if the stories Aslan told her about me were true! She related all kinds of sexual transgressions that I had supposedly done.

Aslan often waited near a subway entrance to catch me when I emerged. I'd hurry away to avoid him. He'd catch up and grab my arm, "It' all a mistake, what I did was wrong. Give me a kiss and let's make love," he said.

I'd tear my arm away and tell him, "Our relationship is over. It's over."

"It can't be!" he'd say and rush to catch and stop me again.

I was terrified to walk my dog in the evenings. I became afraid traveling to work. One afternoon Aslan showed up at my office. He demanded, "Take me back!"

I asked my secretary, a former Army sergeant, to keep watch in case Aslan tried to harm me.

I filed restraining orders against him and actually handed them to him when he appeared. It was a dreadful situation.

I kept a diary after Aslan left. It documents months of his frightening actions, from calls in the middle of the night to stalking me as I returned from work or shopping.

One Sunday afternoon, a nursing colleague, Mary D... and I

went out. We returned to my apartment for dinner. After we arrived, the doorbell rang. Two policemen were at the door inquiring if everything was all right. Aslan had called the police, stating that he was married and that I was entertaining a man in the apartment. Neither my friend nor I wanted to eat after that episode. I was embarrassed that something like that happened. I'm glad we are still the best of friends.

During the five years we were married, Aslan claimed he couldn't find a job. However, after he left, he quickly found one through recommendations of comrades from his home country.

Chapter Twenty One

SAVED BY ANOTHER DOCTOR

In that summer of 1995, a mammogram at Lennox Hill Hospital showed a lump in my breast. It had been there for years. A doctor reviewed the old films and said the edge of the lump appeared to be radiating outward more than previously. He thought I should have a lumpectomy. I thought it was not a big deal. I wore a 34 DD bra and could lose a little breast fat.

I couldn't find the doctor I wanted. I wanted the head of surgery at St. Vincent's Hospital where I had worked in the 1970's. The doctor from Lennox Hill called me every other day, prompting me to find another surgeon. After three weeks, he suggested another surgeon at St. Vincent's Hospital. I decided to go with his recommendation.

Because the lump was flat like a dish, a radiologist took an X-ray before the surgery and stuck a thin wire needle through the lump to where it ended. The needle guides the surgeon where to stop cutting. What I didn't know then, when the radiologist stuck the needle into my breast, he felt a tough part within the lump. He cautioned me, "Don't touch the needle." The pathology of the lump was negative, but that tough part in the center was a non-breast cancer most likely something toxic I had been exposed to when I was a girl. The surgeon didn't know what it might have been.

"So, the mammograms are negative. I don't have to do anything," I told the surgeon.

"That's true, Alexandra. But that cancer inside the lump was invasive, meaning the cancer cells have travelled away from the main site," the doctor said.

I was shocked. "I'll get back to you," I said and left. I was overwhelmed with grief. The summer day was clear and bright. The sun shone on my face as if nothing in my world had really changed. But it had.

I walked gazing at New York City as if I had never seen it before. I continued until dusk, when I arrived at my apartment building. Nothing mattered anymore. I had cancer and I could die soon. The cancer was invasive and had probably hit my blood stream sending out scouts to metastasize. I envisioned little gray cells opening up their mouths and blowing cancer seeds throughout my body. I asked God for some guidance. I was afraid and didn't know what best to do. I had options. I had several choices: surgery, radiation, chemotherapy and doing nothing. I knew I must do something. I had breastfed all my children. At that time, my breasts were my friends, and now they weren't my friends anymore.

I went to work the next day in my medical unit at a brokerage firm. Part of my job was to clear people returning to work after an illness. A chubby woman returning after her bout with breast cancer came in. She had opted for chemotherapy in lieu of surgery. She related the horrors of her chemotherapy.

She had a toxic reaction from the treatment. All her hair fell out, including her eyelashes, and she almost died of pneumonia because she had no resistance to infection. She was treated with cortisone to counteract the symptoms of the chemotherapy. This caused her to puff up like a toad. The company had provided a cab for her to go to her treatments from work. She cried as she related that only one fellow worker was kind to her during the times she was being treated. Other workers shunned her as if they might catch the cancer. She had convinced her doctor to let her come back sooner than she had recommended because she was afraid of losing her job. Her pale lips quivered as she said, "I'm finally back." I had not recognized her at first, but I suddenly recalled how she looked before her illness. I was shocked at her change. I told her that she could come and rest in my office anytime.

There it was. I was not opting for chemotherapy. That night I prayed with my hands on my breast searching for an answer. Just have them both breasts off, I thought. It was more than a thought. It was a directive. I thought pensively about that. I made a decision. That's it! I'm not going to have chemotherapy, radiation or plastic surgery. I will have them off.

I returned to the surgeon with the option to have them both off.

"That's prudent," he said. I asked if he ever had a case like mine before. He had. One patient who had both breasts off, was a tennis professional. She died years later of kidney cancer that was unrelated. I asked if the insurance would pay for removing both breasts and he said he thought so.

My friends suggested I visit a plastic surgeon and explore reconstruction. I did. At the time saline implants were popular. One drawback was that they could leak on impact. Since I was still bicycling, the idea of a crash and an implant going splat stopped me from getting them. I didn't want to worry about that!

It is not easy to tell your children that you are having both breasts off when only one apparently has cancer. My son, Ming, who was in New Mexico, argued with me for hours over the phone. He didn't think it was a prudent decision. He said, "You have too much faith in the doctor."

"I do and that is why he's going to take both off," I said.

I told him," My breasts were once my friends and they're not my friends anymore." He later told me that was the dumbest thing I ever said.

Although the operation was grueling, some things were

amusing.

After the operation, I was kept in the recovery room until 6 p.m. because there were no available hospital rooms. Every so often, a nurse would come and shoot me in the leg with a pain killer. I overheard two doctors making rounds and my name, "Alex."

"It went into the lung," one of them said.

"How do you know that?" asked the other.

"We took a flat plate in the operating room," he responded meaning an X-ray.

Hearing this propelled me into groggy God talk. "Ok, so I didn't call you personally. I thought you'd understand. I didn't bargain for..." And then I dozed off again.

Then the nurses, "Alex, move. Alex, move. Oh, look at all that blood." Reeling with pain and dumb from medicine, I managed to sit up and look around.

"What? What?" I groaned.

"No, not you, him," she bellowed and pointed to the next bed.

In a bed next to me was a man handcuffed to the bed rail. This was another Alex, who had been shot in the chest. Chest tubes were draining his blood. "Thanks, God." I whispered and fell back to sleep.

After getting into a room, I spent three days watching television loops of ponds, lakes, ducks and other meditative scenes. The spacious room was on the top floor of the hospital with a view of the Hudson River. It was a V.I.P. room saved for sick priests and nuns. I thought I must be special.

A priest came to my bedside and prayed. I guessed he was fresh from India because of his accent. He made the sign of the cross and spoke incoherently. He quickly turned and bolted out the door.

That was scary, I thought. I didn't know whether I had gotten the last rites or just a healing prayer. Perhaps he had assumed I was a nun. I'll never know.

A visit from a woman volunteer gave me a net brassiere and two falsies. She showed me how to use them. Like I didn't know? I thanked her and played with the bra, trying to decide if I ever wanted to use it. Next, a woman came and demonstrated arm exercises so I wouldn't develop tendon contractures. She too, had a breast removed. I stared to see if I could guess that she had. Was she even? I couldn't tell.

I have never been one for saying I'm a survivor. Anyone who drives a car on a major highway, and lives to tell about it, is a survivor. I think some people with a history of cancer get stuck bonding to other cancer survivors. In my opinion it's tribal. I wanted to continue my life with what I had left. Maybe, if I was married at the time of my mastectomies, I might have regarded my breasts as something to share. Living alone, I didn't have the obligation to share my body parts.

As I write this, it's been eighteen years after the breast affair, and I'm OK. I didn't choose plastic surgery, chemotherapy or radiation. I know this sounds queer, but I believe death might actually be exciting. I don't know how I came into being, so I don't worry about death.

Whatever my children might have thought about my decision to have both my breasts off, in the end I was the genius. Both breasts had multiple cancerous tumors in the milk ducts, in spite of negative mammograms. I was given a new lease on life.

Two weeks after my operation, a nurse friend called.

"How are you?"

"Fine."

"Do you miss them?"

"No."

"Don't you wonder where they went?'

"No."

"Did you join a support group?"

"No."

"I think you're in denial."

"Denial! Every time I take a shower, they're not there. Look, I wasn't attached. I don't have the weight of 34 DDs on my shoulders. It's OK."

"Oh, I was just wondering."

Sadly, Aslan continued to stalk me when I was shopping or exiting the subway. Each time he asked to return and always wanted money. He said he needed more to live. (Over the course of five years, I had given him over forty thousand dollars, more than half of my savings at the time)

After my operation, I still received many letters from Aslan. I either discarded them or sent them back unopened. He still telephoned me frequently during the night and I still left the phone receiver off. I never knew when he would suddenly appear to ask, "Honey why can't we be together?" Each time, because I was fearful, I politely responded that our relationship was over.

I had put his belongings in storage and mailed him the key. He said he wanted me to keep paying the storage because he wanted to visit his mother first and take his things out when he returned. I paid for two more months. That was the last payment for him.

He stalked me past Christmas of 1995 and during the spring of 1996.

My follow-up medical appointments for my mastectomies were finished. I was healthy.

I had endured enough of Aslan and his shenanigans.

An artist friend lived in Taos, New Mexico. She said I should move to Taos and I would have a better life among artists. She found a small duplex I might rent. Dogs were welcome. I called the owner and asked if he wanted money up front.

"No, you sound like a nice lady. Just come on out," he said.

He was my kind of people! I offered my New York apartment to my daughter Tsao Lin and her husband, Emelio. They accepted.

In June, my dog and I began our trip to Taos. The movers were traveling with my hundred-plus paintings and a few pieces of furniture. I had a cell phone for the first time and roadside service in case my car broke down. It was the best life decision I had made so far.

Chapter Twenty Two

TAOS, NEW MEXICO

I was hot and tired traveling with my dog, Pueblo. My small VW 'golf.' was stuffed with precious oil paints, clothes and food. I had arrived! The little duplex I rented was built in the early 1940's. It was my fantasy fulfilled. Hollyhocks were everywhere. The scent of sagebrush blanketed the place after a rain. Everything was fresh and new. Little bugs with red behinds crawled on the doorsteps. The landlord said they were adobe bugs. The house was small but had a fireplace and a fenced yard with grass. My dog liked that. I managed to stack most of my paintings in the bedroom and behind a couch in the living room.

The fact that I had escaped from Aslan made me happy beyond my own belief. Everything was beautiful and enticing. The huge azure sky, people wearing cowboy boots and hats were all welcome to my hungry eyes. I told my landlord that I was escaping an ex-husband who had been stalking me. He said, "Just let him come here. We'll blow him away," meaning he and his friends had firearms.

Since my nursing license for New Mexico had not been processed yet, I explored areas outside Taos painting subjects. I packed the car with water, paints, canvas and of course my dog, and drove out to paint.

I searched for a gallery and was quickly accepted into a local one. New Masters, on Paseo del Norte in Taos exhibited good paintings by competent artists.

I also began working at a Taos trading post owned by

Jackie Baca. She found out from one of my neighbors that my money was running low and hired me part time. I learned about types of turquoise from different mines, pawn jewelry and Indian carved animal fetishes. The fetishes are meant to lure an animal's power to those who possess them. A small carved frog might represent fertility, so a woman who wants to become pregnant might carry this fetish. With the frog fetish, others are not supposed to touch the frog for various reasons. Other fetishes, such as mountain lions or bears are used for hunting. The Zuni Native Americans have fetishes for the six directions.

Jackie bought several of my paintings, so I had food money for the time being.

After I received my New Mexico nursing license, I began work at a local private retirement facility that had a skilled nursing unit. Working there was uncomplicated because very ill residents were sent to the hospital. I soon realized that the owners had little medical background. They didn't know the difference between a practical nurse and a registered nurse! Although the residents were appreciative, the owners were condescending to their employees. I believe the owners acted in this manner because they thought themselves superior because they had money. I had experienced diverse types of wealthy people and I had little difficulty identifying the owners as nouveau riche with an appetite for power.

Next, I worked at a corporate nursing home in Taos. That was the first time I had ever clocked in and out as a professional nurse. Now many employers want their employees to use a time clock. Pay is based on exact minutes of work within the hour. Workers are not allowed to clock in more than ten minutes before a workday or clock out more than ten minutes after their designated hours of work. If they do, the employer has to pay for the extra time.

Professional nurses previously worked until their work was finished. If perchance they worked more than an hour overtime, a supervisor would sign a slip to compensate them for extra money. The nurses I knew didn't care about being compensated for ten minutes here or there.

We often arrived early to work to check patient charts for changes or review the charts of new patients. By arriving early, we gave better care. As nurses, we were concerned more about the care we gave to our patients more than a few minutes here or there. Our patients belonged to us and were our charges. All hospitals gave nurses and nurse aids four weeks' vacation and twelve holidays through the 1990s. We were compensated and were able to accrue vacation days for the next year when we could have eight weeks vacation! One nurse from Kings County Hospital accrued an entire year, and traveled to Europe for a year.

It's my sad opinion that today professional nurses are treated like blue collar workers. Hospitals treat their employees as though they intend to be dishonest. Professional nurses now work in scrubs just like the orderlies who empty the garbage and mop the floors. Patients' respect for nurses has diminished because of this. I will add that nurses graduating today don't know how well nurses were once treated and were continued to be treated until about twenty years ago.

Because I could practice few nursing skills at the nursing home, I sought work at Holy Cross Hospital in Taos. I found it to be a good hospital although much smaller than the three-hundred-bed-plus ones with which I was familiar. I called to arrange a work interview.

"What floor are you on?" I naively asked.

There was a long pause on the other end before the woman said, "Just come on down."

The hospital had only one floor and had a forty-two patient capacity.

I continued to work at the trading post while working at the hospital. One of my male patients had a broken leg. When I entered his room his wife exclaimed, "Why here's the woman from the trading post."

"Yes, I have more than one job here in Taos. I'm also a registered nurse," I said.

Sometimes I felt like an impostor because some patients had the notion that you had to work at just one occupation to be good at that. It seemed silly to have to defend myself. Later, I had similar responses in the hospital because I also worked at La Tierra Mineral Gallery, which was a rock shop.

While I was working in Labor and Delivery at Holy Cross, a couple couldn't decide on a name for their baby girl. I said jokingly, while holding up my name tag, "I always liked my name, Alexandra."

The next day when I returned, the grandmother leapt up and squeezed me.

She said, "We named her after you, Alexandra. You are such a wonderful nurse!"

Not even my granddaughter is named after me! What a thrill. I sopped up adulations that followed.

After a couple of years working in Taos, I bought a house on Holly Circle with a huge backyard and managed to acquire three dogs. My house was near a grammar school. Several kids, on their way home, frequently climbed up at the side of my fence to throw rocks at the dogs. My daughter, Tzu Ling, who was visiting at the time, suggested I write the dogs' biographies and attach them to the fence. That way it might appeal to the children's kindness.

I copied pictures of the dogs with a brief history and put each into a plastic sleeve and nailed them to the fence at the side walkway. It worked. The children read the biographies then peered through the fence to identify which dog belonged to the picture on the fence.

I liked Taos because people were friendly. When I first arrived I didn't have a job. People who knew I wasn't working left fruit on my doorstep.

Taos Art Association was supportive, but the art community was not as supportive as I had hoped. I found the artists I met were protective of their successes. Most had not had a formal art education and were limited in their ability. They stuck to a painterly niche if they were able to sell. For myself, I can look at a painting and know if it is contrived or not. I do not mean that every good artist must have a formal education. An artist who paints with sincerity and has the true art spirit makes all the difference in the world.

My experience of artists in New York City had been different. Artists I met had been glad to help one another. We chatted about colors, new oil paints and products and what shows were worth seeing as well as competitions or shows I or others might enter.

Eventually, the Taos gallery in which I was showing had money problems and closed. I continued to work at Holy Cross Hospital for several years before moving to Albuquerque.

While living in New Mexico I worked at various nursing jobs, some at local Indian reservations and others at a hospital. Although I was successful at nursing, and it had been a means of support, I never warmed to nursing as some nurses do. It never enveloped me like painting and writing. I am grateful that I had the opportunity help people and that I had the brains to excel, but it was never a "fit."

The move to New Mexico in 1996 was a good decision. It provided relief from being stalked by Aslan as well as the breast cancer episode. It was a new page of my life– a new page away from tragic marriages and memories.

Good things happen when you are brave enough to make a decision, or as I sometimes say, "Take a decision."

In 2011, when I became seventy years old, I finally gave up nursing for painting and writing.

As it stands, I have not had a relationship or lived with a man since 1996 when I was cured of marriage. Living alone has given me a chance to explore my life's purpose and practice Buddhism.

Chapter Twenty Three

BUDDHISM?

I was still working in Labor and Delivery at Holy Cross Hospital in 2001. One of the nurses with whom I worked, mentioned that she met with a Tibetan monk in Santa Fe. She had wanted spiritual advice.

She turned and said, "You should go to Santa Fe and see him. He's quite interesting and not at all imposing."

Hmm, I thought. Perhaps I might go there. The stupa, as she called the temple on Airport Road, was easily found because of its unusual shape sprouting from the flat terrain. I made an appointment with the resident Lama. Lama Karma Dorje belonged to the Tibetan Kagyu sect. I asked what I might bring to the Lama as a token of appreciation. A friend, Marj S. from Taos drove with me. I took twenty pounds of bird seed as a gift. I had been told Lama Dorje had a small aviary and liked birds.

He wore a burgundy robe over a bright yellow silk shirt. Our meeting seemed quite ordinary. He asked about my children and my work. Upon parting, he gave me a mantra to recite– "O" "Mani Padme Hum." Saying the mantra invokes the benevolence and blessing of Chenrezig/Avalokiteshvera, the embodiment of compassion of all the Buddhas, the Bodhisattva of Compassion.

In the Buddhist shop, I bought a small blue disk on a cord, supposedly for protection. As I opened the door to my truck, I used such force, the door bashed into my head. Ouch! My friend, Marj laughed and said, "Hey, I thought that thing was supposed to protect you!"

I thought I better pay attention to what I'm doing, like driving home carefully.

I recited the mantra for several weeks without any noticeable change. My neck had become stiff and quite painful. I thought I should visit the Lama and tell him about my neck. Perhaps I wasn't reciting the mantra properly. I drove to Santa Fe again. Lama Dorje was out in the yard, looking up at a tree. As I approached, I saw several birds hopping about on the low branches. They were either nuthatches or chickadees.

I told him about my neck problem and moved my head from side to side several times to make my point. At first the monk thought I was talking about the birds with their black necks. Suddenly, he glared at me and I knew he understood. His look had such strength, I could not talk. I tried to say something, but couldn't utter a word. I stood transfixed and remembered a phrase from Job in the Old Testament— "and their tongues cleaved to the roof of their mouths."

The Lama said, "Come with me."

He rushed me into the adjacent Buddhist shop and inquired, "Where's Medicine Buddha? Where's the mantra for Medicine Buddha?"

A woman handed him a small, blue folded card which he handed to me. A mantra and a picture were printed on opposite sides.

He started to leave but stopped and said, "Oh, I have to empower you."

After saying that, he placed his left hand on my shoulder and pointed his right hand up as if pointing at the sky. He recited something in Tibetan, then turned and said, "say the mantra 10,000 times and your neck will be better," and left!

Stunned, I turned to the book shelf and spied a blue book entitled, Medicine Buddha-Restricted. I asked the woman employee if I could buy it.

She answered, "Oh yes, you can buy it, if you've been empowered. I never saw anyone empowered so fast in my life."

I bought the book. When I returned home, I began a daily practice of Medicine Buddha. That was my beginning as a Buddhist.

After visiting Lama Dorje several times, he asked, "Why don't you visit the Lama in El Rito, it's north of Questa–Lama Chodrak? He's very near you."

He gave me Lama Chodrak's telephone number to make an appointment. I called a few days later and made one for 4 p.m.

When I drove to meet Lama Chodrak it was a cold, blustery afternoon in early spring. Snow had melted in some areas. I steered my car onto a muddy road to the front of the colorful stupa building. I realized this small building was not where the Lama lived. I tried to backup but my car quickly sank into the muddy ground. I slipped out from my car onto the mud. I sloshed onto the driveway as a man emerged from a nearby pop-up trailer. He had been on retreat. He informed me that Lama Chodrak was in a house up the road. My breath steamed before my face as I trekked up for my appointment.

Lama Chodrak greeted me and ushered me into an altar room with many statues of buddhas and lighted candles. He was perhaps in his thirties and wore the Kagyu traditional robes– a dark red skirt and red material draped over his left shoulder which partly covered a sleeveless yellow silk shirt. I made three prostrations in front of the Buddhist altar before I spoke. Wearily, I told the lama about where my car was stuck in the mud.

"Very auspicious," he calmly replied.

He wasn't concerned about my dilemma at all. He asked me to sit and offered tea and asked why I wanted to visit. I talked about how my Buddhist practice was progressing and asked him questions I had written down.

The afternoon light was getting darker toward evening. I had the nightmarish thought that I would never get my car unstuck until the next day. It was nearly dark when the lama got up from his chair and telephoned someone for help.

"Oh, Hi. A visitor's car is stuck in front of the stupa. Can you come help?" He asked.

Lama Chodrak and I walked to my car by the stupa. We met a man with a truck and a rope.

The man took a look and said, "I don't know if I can get you out, because your car is sideways to the road. I might get stuck too."

The lama looked from the truck to my car and back again. He closed his eyes as if in prayer. Little by little I got unstuck. Snow was beginning to fall as I turned my car onto the highway. Auspicious I thought, very auspicious.

Since 2001, I have practiced Tibetan Buddhism. Like most of my life, important changes came in unusual ways.

A few years ago, I drove to Santa Fe to visit Lama Dorje, the lama who had introduced me to Buddhism and my spiritual practice. I entered his small room. Much to my surprise, there were two other lamas, Lama Chodrak and Lama Chopal. I greeted Lama Dorje and said, "How good can it get? Here I am in a room with three lamas."

Lama Dorje held out a plate with candies, and said, "How about a piece of chocolate?"

I practice as best I can. The meditative practice of taming one's mind has helped me. My mind still needs a little taming.

Chapter Twenty Four

PUEBLO AND WALTER

Before I moved to Taos, I found a wonderful dog at the North Shore Animal Shelter in Long Island. I had put my aged Brittany Spaniel down the day before. He had a failing heart. The next day, drove to the shelter and looked for another dog. Because I had a cat, I wanted a gentle dog. I was sobbing as I peered into the cages.

One woman worker said, "Madam, you're not ready for a dog."

"Yes I am!" I said, "James Herriot says so." – the pen name for James Alfred Wight, the Scottish veterinarian, who wrote *All Creatures Great and Small.*

I told the woman he said, "People who lose a dog should get another one right away."

I looked at several dogs before one caught my eye. It was a dog with pale blue eyes, possibly part Dalmatian and Lab. I said I wanted to see the dog.

Another worker said, "That dog don't always take kindly to people, he's been abused and the police took him from someone."

I asked, "What did they do to him?"

He responded, "You wouldn't want to know!"

But, this blue eyed dog had given me–that look.

The look that speaks, "I've been waiting here for you."

I told the worker I wanted to see him anyway.

North Shore Shelter had a large room with a spacious, four-sided bench in the middle. Prospective dog owners had the opportunity to sit at a side with a dog. My future dog sat quietly while I patted his head. After about a half hour he turned and stood up on the side of the bench to give me a kiss on my cheek.

I said, "Now if I take you, it's forever."

I wanted to own him, but the shelter required recommendations. Cell phones didn't exist. Each friend I tried calling was working. In desperation I called my veterinarian and received a good report. I got my dog.

It was February and the temperature was well below freezing when I arrived back to my apartment on Gold Street.

I walked the dog. He wouldn't pee. I took him to the nearby dog park. He ignored the other dogs, and still didn't pee. He didn't pee after dinner. I went to bed and to sleep. Sometime in the night I awoke. He was staring at me with his head very close to my face.

I remembered the shelter worker's words, "That dog don't always take kindly to people."

What in hell did I do? I don't know anything about this dog. A cold fear spread over my body.

I said, "Go lie down." He did.

The next day was better. He managed to pee and perform other bodily functions. We played ball under a Brooklyn Bridge Arch. After each throw and catch, at which he was very good, he'd drop the ball at my feet.

I had found a good dog but, soon after I got him, he broke off my front tooth. One Saturday, while playing ball, he ran straight into my face. He did not knock out my tooth but broke it at the root. It was a weekend. My dentist was away, but, he had a substitute. When I called, he told me the dog couldn't possible have broken my tooth off; it was probably just knocked out a little and could be stuck back into the gum. He couldn't see me until Monday.

"I'm so, so sorry. I've never seen a tooth broken off like this," the dentist said on Monday.

"Let's see if I can put a screw into the root and cap it with matching porcelain. That's just what he did. It cost about eight hundred dollars.

I named the dog Pueblo because he reminded me of dogs I had seen out west on Native American reservations.

Pueblo was a good traveler and liked to ride in cars. He wasn't a lap dog, nor was he nervous. He'd stare into people's eyes when they greeted me. A nurse friend thought he seemed like a person who died and returned as a dog. He traveled with me to Taos when I moved from New York City.

In Taos, my small duplex was a block away from The Best Western Kachina Lodge. Native American entertainers played on weekends for their guests. If there was a breeze, I could hear faint chanting. One evening, Pueblo stood at the cellar door and growled. He was determined to tell me something was amiss. I wondered if someone was in the cellar. Perhaps a previous renter had a key. With a pot in hand for a weapon, I nervously opened the cellar door. The black chasm of the cellar, once illuminated revealed nothing but the stairs. After shutting the metal-covered door, I felt it with my hand. The metal vibrated from the entertainers' chants and drums. I opened the door again, so Pueblo could peer into the cellar.

"See, no one's there," I said. "Are you trying to give me a heart attack?"

A year had passed and it was February once again. I had Pueblo for a year. On a trip to Wal-Mart, I found another dog I named Walter, in memory of our hired farmhand. A year after that, in 1999, I found another wonderful dog, Tuba.

Pueblo and Walter lived until 2008. Pueblo was thirteen and

Walter was eight. Pueblo, Walter and Tuba had many years of fun together.

Chapter Twenty Five

A Memory of Tuba

In August 2012, I moved to California. I didn't stay, but I'm getting ahead of myself. As I was packing, I noticed my little, black Tuba dog had trouble walking up the few steps to my apartment. He had grown thin and weak over the past few weeks. A friend commented that perhaps he didn't want to move to California. Sadly, the day before my move, I had to put little Tuba to sleep. He had been my companion for thirteen years.

I found Tuba way out in the desert. In 1999, Rhoda, an editor and good friend from New York, came to visit me in Taos, New Mexico. I had just bought the house on Holly Circle. We decided to take a trip to the Grand Canyon and Monument Valley. I drove, because Rhoda didn't. My other dogs, Pueblo and Walter were staying with a neighbor. I drove to the Albuquerque airport and picked up Rhoda. We started out immediately. My car began to lose speed. We crept along with continuous spurts of acceleration and finally made it to Gallup, New Mexico that night. The next morning a faulty spark plug was found to be the culprit.

We were soon speeding along to meet up with Rhoda's friends at the Grand Canyon. After a view of the sunrise and a quick breakfast, Rhoda and I started for Monument Valley and Canyon de Chelly. I was irritable. Alert driving and a stiff neck made me testy. The hot sun was beating down as we passed Tuba City, Arizona. The town was named for Chief Tuba, a Hopi leader in the 19th century.

Highway 160 to Kayenta was a two-lane uneventful road. Dirt bluffs and a few trees marked our route. Driving required tedious concentration because the road was boring and the air was hot as a frying pan. Rhoda looked at travel brochures as I clipped along. I saw a tiny, black spot, out of the corner of my eye, whiz by. A dog! I quickly checked the rear view mirror and reversed the car on the sandy shoulder.

"What's happening? What are you doing?" Rhoda cried out.

Oh my! On the hot sand stood a tiny hairless, sore-ridden dog. He teetered on his small feet as he looked up at us. He looked more like a rat than a dog.

After a snack of brie and a drink of water, he collapsed on a towel Rhoda had spread on her lap. The next stop was at a hamburger mart in Kayenta. Standing by the car, the dog greedily ate a hamburger. A woman approached, after viewing us, and asked if we needed a veterinarian. She told us there was an animal Indian Health Service nearby. At first the technician didn't want to see the dog, because they did paperwork in the afternoon. Rhoda and I sat and waited determinately to see the doctor. Eventually a very pleasant veterinarian emerged from the back. He weighed the dog, examined his ears and eyes and listened to his heart. He gave us pills and Frontline spray for his mange and scabies. What was the dog's name?

"Why it's Tuba." We had both decided. Since Rhoda and I were used to New York veterinarian prices; we thought the bill was going to be at least a hundred dollars. Much to our relief and surprise it was only eighteen.

This was the beginning of Tuba, who was found on the Navajo Nation in Tuba City, Arizona. Over the years he had a wonderful life with several other dog companions. He was the only dog who always minded me. Nights when I couldn't sleep, I'd read poetry to him. A sleepy eye would open and close as if to say, "Go on, I'm still listening."

Chapter Twenty Six

CALIFORNIA

In May, 2012, My son, Ming, the oldest moved to California and married a woman who had a house in El Cajon. After the marriage, he and his wife bought a spacious, upscale house with a swimming pool in Escondido, California. I was still living in Albuquerque, New Mexico.

He called and said "Hey, why don't you move to California and live in my wife's house. I'll pay for the move." This was in August.

That sounded great to me. I thought of all the nice things in California like the beach, the zoo and the redwood forest, to name a few. In two weeks I had packed my belongings and crated a hundred of my paintings in thick cardboard. I taped them with Gorilla Tape. I love Gorilla Tape. I worked furiously to finish, because my son had said that the house would be free in the middle of August and that he would like me there soon, so the house wouldn't be empty for a long time. Although my son loves me and was generous in paying for my move, the move wasn't a fit. First of all, I had not seen the house when I attended my son's wedding in May. That was my big mistake.

When I arrived in California gas was much too expensive at $5.35 a gallon. Since my good friend from New York lived eighty miles away and my son and wife were thirty eight miles away, visiting wasn't going to be often.

Also, Californians are maniacs behind the wheel. They charge out like calves from a rodeo shoot. They don't look to the side to see if another car is there – like using the corner of their eye. They look straight ahead as if they are on a conveyor belt, possibly caused by too much computer screen staring. One good thing about their driving is that they are just driving. They are definitely not texting on their cell phones or putting on makeup like they do here in New Mexico, or eating a Big Mac and sipping a Big Slurp. They are smart enough to know they will be road kill if they do and be gobbled up by the roof rats that are waiting at the side of the road—more about them later.

If I visited my friend in Laguna Hills which was eighty miles away, I had to leave early in the morning and start back before 2 p.m.; otherwise the traffic would be so congested that it would take me four hours to get home.

First of all, I was worried about my dog, Madeleine, an English Bulldog. She can not tolerate a lot of heat. When I drove through Quartzsite, Arizona on my way to California, the temperature was 109 degrees. I prayed that I would not break down, because Madeleine and I would be dead. When I reached El Cajon it was over 104 degrees. The house had a portable air conditioner, the kind you wheel around from room to room. I spent a week in one room with my dog while I waited for the movers.

After a week and a half, my son put in central air condition. In California they don't call it air conditioning.

They just call it air. "Do you have air?"

There are often language differences. When you thank them, they don't say "You're welcome." They say, "No problem."

Did I give them a problem? Californians say this because everything in California is so expensive and this is the problem that's on everyone's mind. They have to keep reassuring themselves that there are no problems.

Since I am on a very limited, fixed income, every cost was a nightmare. I will not bore you about the cost of the house utilities, car insurance, my driver's license test, or car registration. I got a break from my son renting the house, but I couldn't even pay that. Everything cost, cost, cost.

My Bulldog got fleas. Frontline does not work on the Californian fleas. It's too cheap a product. There is something more expensive called Comfortis. I found that out from my first veterinarian visit. I suspect they calculate the price of flea medication by using the cost index of gas. Let's see, the cost of gas, $5.35 times 26 gives you $140. That means the flea medication was worth approximately 26 gallons of gas and vice versa. Depending what number the vet likes, next week it might be 30 because that will be the calendar date of your visit. And the medication will be $160.50.

Madeleine's belly blew up with an infection from the flea bites. It cost me $140.00 for the medication—guaranteed to cure, because the price of gas held at $5.35 and the vet liked the number 26.

El Cajon not only has a different kind of flea, it has a different kind of rat. (I'm not joking.) It is a roof rat. These rats run along the high tension wires outside your house like monkeys. When they get to an electrical line leading to your house they run right to it and set up housekeeping in your attic! They also make nests in the tall cedar trees that line the side streets of El Cajon. I had only one rat. I found it outside in the garage area near the garbage container. My dog found it for me. It was dead and had been killed by California fleas.

Mice also liked the house. They were cute little things that knew all about traps, except one mouse which got squashed on the kitchen counter. They must have a wise, old teacher mouse who sits under the kitchen sink. He tells the little mice not to go near the cheese or the bacon.

"Go directly to the cereal and raisins up on the shelves. Nibble a little sugar or soap while you're at it. Now, off you go!"

I heard the mice laughing at night. They had a very small TV behind the washing machine in the hall where they watched Tom and Jerry Netflix movies. Well, I'm joking of course because I was trying to put a good face on a bad situation.

Aside from the mice, rats and fleas, I was lonely. The house was nice but I had no writer friends. All my friends were in New Mexico. I did not take to the locals and wanted to go back to Albuquerque. I had given California about six months. My son, who is very generous, paid for my move back to my old apartment house. Luckily, there was a vacant apartment.

California was not all bad. It was another learning experience, and a good one. I learned I will never move to a place that I have not checked out first. That the exchange of ideas is important to my mental health and creative spirit. I concluded that I couldn't live in California on a meager, fixed income and that the rats and fleas there are mutants that were transported to El Cajon by maniac drivers who don't text.

Chapter Twenty Seven

CHILDREN

My relationships with my children

are tenuous and not what I had hoped for. If I lived closer to them, perhaps I wouldn't be so isolated and we'd have more interaction. My two sons, Ming and Tai, are closer; they tell me, "I love you too," when I tell them I love them. Tai and his wife, Tara, have my wonderful grandson, Jonah. They live in New York City. When I call, Jonah is eager to talk. What a joy!

My son Ming who now lives in California, became closer to me when he moved to Albuquerque where I live also. He got to know how I have changed since he left for college in the 1980s.

My daughters, Tzu Ling and Tsao Lin, are more distant. I haven't heard the words "I love you" from them in years. Why? I would like to converse with them to repair our relationships.

When I call my oldest daughter, Tsao Lin, she answers the phone asking, "What's up?"

She'll call on my birthday and on other holidays, "Oh happy... bye-bye."

I know little about her life and my granddaughter, Isabella. I was on FaceBook once and saw that Tsao Lin and the family were going on a vacation to France. Both my daughters are very busy. I may hear from Tsao Lin once a year, maybe on Mother's Day.

My youngest daughter hasn't called me in years. On a rare occasion she might answer her phone if I call.

Every six months or so, I call and leave a message, " Hi Tzu,

I've been thinking of you and wondering how you're doing. I hope everything is going well...I love you. Take care, it's Mother."

I wrote letters to Tzu Ling, and found out in 2008, on my sixty-seventh birthday that she never opens them. I wrote what happened then:

October 23, 2008:

Today is a special day for me. It is my birthday and I am sixty-seven years old. I am back in my old stomping grounds in New York City, about to go with my daughter to the Metropolitan Museum of Art. The air is cool with a brisk breeze. Small scraps of paper are swirling down the street as I look out the apartment window.

I can hardly wait to see my beautiful daughter, Tzu Ling, who now is a doctor at a New York hospital. She meets me at Tsao's apartment. She's dressed in a green jacket and a red muffler that's wrapped around her neck. She gives me a quick hug. I am so happy to reunite with her. We walk to Chinatown and buy some pastries and coffee to snack on the way to the museum. We sit outside the museum by a fountain and enjoy the food, but she seems distant at my enthusiasm to see her. I think it is probably because I have been living in New Mexico for several years and don't get back to New York very often. We go up the steps and notice a sign that forbids food or drink inside, so we leave the bag with an extra pastry on a ledge for a hungry person to eat.

I am excited as always, to visit the paintings here. We roam around for a couple of hours and leave for lunch. Tzu suggests a nearby restaurant called EAT. It is the same restaurant where I ate lunch on my sixty-fifth birthday! I had also gone to the Metropolitan Museum of Art then as a birthday present for myself.

We sit at a small table for two. Toward the end of our lunch, Tzu hands me a piece of paper with names and phone numbers.

She says, "I think you should see a psychiatrist. These are very good doctors and one is in Rio Rancho." (the city in New Mexico where I now live).

I am taken aback. She says, "I think you are manic and when I talk to you on the phone, you seem hyper and I think you might benefit from some medication too."

I tell her, "I am seeing a Jungian therapist, Dr. C. because I had a compelling dream in which I passed out."

Tzu looks at me in a concerned way before getting up. I don't know what to say. I feel rejected. We catch a downtown bus to 14th Street. Tzu wants to buy me a pair of nice shoes. It seems like a distraction or an apology for the critical way she perceives me. I am racing my mind to remember what I did or said that compels her to see me in this light.

She happily buys me an expensive pair of black leather shoes that have been designed by two women doctors. We board a downtown bus once again.

I ask, "Did you get the letter I sent?"

She says, "I never open your letters. I just put them in a drawer and keep them for posterity."

I ask, "Why is that?"

She tells me she is too upset by my letters to open them. It is the same for packages. I am devastated, but say nothing. I want to cry, but don't because I am on the bus. She suddenly pulls the cord to exit.

She gets up and says, "I'm going to stop by Dad's office. I have some things to pick up."

She gives me a quick kiss on the cheek. I watch her go out at the front of the bus. She turns and waves as I continue to my other daughter Tsao Lin's apartment, an apartment I gave to her when I moved to New Mexico.

I have just finished dinner at Tsao's. I am settled in and ready for bed. I plan to read a little first. My granddaughter has given up her bedroom for me and has been sleeping in her parents' room. She is a lovey.

A telephone call from my son Ming to wish me happy birthday. But it is not just that.

He asks, "Did you talk to Tzu?"

"Yes," I say.

"Well what do you think about her suggestion? Did you find out why Tzu did not speak to you for so long?"

"I think she wants me to be ordinary, beige and fade into the wall. She said she is under a lot of stress."

He responds, "Well really it is something else. Tzu and I agree that you get manic. I can hear it in your voice sometimes over the telephone. I think she has a good suggestion. She is sensitive in observing you and didn't she think medication might help you?"

I don't argue with him. I say, "Yes, I should be more ordinary."

I do not challenge him. His former wife had

referred to me as having hare-brained ideas. One was that I thought of going to Ethiopia with an editor friend to help a Canadian doctor set up a medical clinic, since I have done that in the past. There are no emergency medical clinics there. I didn't because Somalia was nearby and it was not safe.

When I was writing a children's story, his wife who read part of it said, "Yeah, there's big words– kids love to look up big words."

I wonder does Emelio, my son-in-law think I am manic?

What a birthday!

I am back in New Mexico and hotfoot it to Dr. C. the Jungian therapist. I relate my New York experience to her:

She exclaims, "Scapegoating! Look it up. These people are scapegoating you. They project things on someone else instead of taking care of their own SHIT!"

It seems this happens frequently in families. Sometimes a member is designated as a "black sheep." Blame is placed on the person in a similar way. I will continue to assess my children and my relationships with them. Thank you Dr. C.

(When I attended nursing school, doctors were cautioned not to diagnose or treat their relatives.)

I must remember not to be so upbeat when I speak to my children on the phone. As a mother, I am always trying not to burden them. I think I shouldn't be too enthusiastic about painting, making jewelry, cooking or other things I do. I should add some bad stuff that's happening in my life, so I don't get classified as "manic."

I love my children and grandchildren dearly. I raised them

to be independent. They are self-sufficient, smart, educated and successful. I must remember though, that they are half their father.

I am saddened by my children's withholding of love. That is an old plague from my past. Maya Angelou said, "You don't own your children, God does."

≈ ≈ ≈ ≈

AFTERWORD

Jungian psychotherapy, painting and writing have made me whole. I am able to review my past objectively and be enthusiastic about my future.

I have been depressed most of my life, but sadness has been a protection. It was a dark mental cloak that enveloped a particular part of my past. It was always with me like a black eddy circling around my soul while my outward life appeared reasonably normal. Although melancholy buried my self esteem, anger, joy and enthusiasm, it helped me survive. It kept the past buried until memories were safe to emerge. The past emerged because of psychotherapy.

The trauma of my past replaced my enthusiasm for life with excitement. I was excited and hopeful of happiness when I married so many times. I had hoped to recapture the happiness of my early life before Stoelting. That happiness I had before I was molested–a feeling of joy and anticipation of what the day might bring.

Any rejection still stings and is tied to my past. The fact that the jury did not believe me about Stoelting, and my father thinking that I had ruined his imagined mission were devastating. He visited me just once when I was in the convent, this furthering my feelings of rejection. The way I was shunned in school and how my relatives changed in the way they treated me reinforced my belief of unworthiness. Rejection is one stain from my past that continues to stab my heart.

My social life started in art school where I made friends. The artists weren't critical. We were too engrossed about what we were creating. The creative process was more important than how much money people had or how they looked. Viewing other artists' work incited us to create more. We gleaned ideas that we might apply to our own work.

The men I married, after my first, were attracted to me like magnets. They said I was great, interesting, smart and sexy. They couldn't wait to get married. I appeased them and got married. At the time the marriages pacified my longing for love. There has always been a sad longing in my life. Perhaps because I had been separated from my mother so many times with the reward of her return. I learned early on how to appease her. I appeased Stoelting in order to survive. I discovered the more I complied with my husbands' wishes, the more unhappy I became.

I was so quick to please these men.

You want me to learn Chinese cooking, sure I can do that. I can even learn to speak Chinese. You want me to go camping? I can do that too.

You say you want me to support your poor family in another country. Why not. That was the last husband, the forth. I did that for five years.

Throughout my life, I have tried to rearrange my world to find happiness. I realized I was damaged in some way. But the crux is that I had never experienced genuine love. I spent most of my life in busyness. Hither and thither I went, always trying different projects to express myself, and at the same time attempting to please my husbands.

I just mention how I complied to point out similarities of the men I chose. They all had the art of snaffling. That is a word that refers to the control of a horse through a metal bit in their mouth. Yat Ting, my first husband, pressured me to give the pearled filigreed bracelet to Dr. Liu who delivered my son because it was a practice of doctors not to charge other doctors. My second husband, Frank begged for money when we divorced. He said, "I don't have a pot to piss in."

I believed it was my responsibility to help others. The savior! I'm sure it was ego driven and propelled by fear, shame and rejection. I falsely believed if I could help a needy man, I would be accepted as a normal, wonderful person, validated and loved. I recognize this now. I am alert to men who want a nurse or a purse.

I am amazed, when I hear how my friends knew as children, that they disagreed with their parents and had ideas of their own. As a child, I was the good one and was never able to question what my mother demanded.

I picked men who were rigid and controlling similar to Stoelting, but certainly not the same. My marriages fell apart each time when I changed. Painting became more joyful than marriage. When I finish a painting, I am filled with self esteem from a tangible object. A painting doesn't reject the artist.

I believe that true love is compassionate, but one has to evaluate and decide if the mate is the right mate.

Although my father didn't want to talk about Stoelting after I returned from the convent, my mother told me that she knew I had saved her life. In retrospect, I don't believe that my father was capable of physically hurting my mother.

In writing my memoir I found the good and the bad were buried together. I relived painful memories and found that good ones popped up later. Writing about my life has made me free. It is truth that lights the world.

About the Author

Alexandra Dell'Amore is a Registered Nurse and holds a degree in Fine Arts Painting. Her nursing career included directing a residential drug rehab program in the Bronx, working with the homeless mentally ill in New York City through a Boston University grant and many other achievements. She has received numerous awards for her painting including a grant from The National Endowment for the Arts. Her work has been featured in many gallery and museum shows and exhibitions, both in New York and in Taos, New Mexico.

Her interest in Jungian psychology and art as well as her experience in the medical field inspired her to write this memoir to tell how her often chaotic life became integrated. She presently lives in New Mexico where she continues to write and paint. She is a member of Southwest Writers.